THE BATTLE
OF THE FITTEST
UNDER THE BLOOD

GLORIA V GRIFFIN

WESTBOW
PRESS®
A DIVISION OF THOMAS NELSON
& ZONDERVAN

WestBow Press books may be ordered through booksellers or by contacting:

WestBow Press
A Division of Thomas Nelson & Zondervan
1663 Liberty Drive
Bloomington, IN 47403
www.westbowpress.com
844-714-3454

ISBN: 979-8-3850-3773-5 (sc)
ISBN: 979-8-3850-3772-8 (e)

Library of Congress Control Number: 2024923246

Print information available on the last page.

WestBow Press rev. date: 11/19/2024

CONTENTS

CONTENTS

PREFACE

I am a Spiritual woman, a child of God, who has walked out of religion into *Sonship with our divine Creator, which means I follow Christ Yeshua [Bible. Romans 8.14]. My decision to write became a reality when He said, "You need to write a book." I could not understand what in my life could be so attractive that people would want to read about it. Writing a biography was never a thought in my mind. This accomplishment took years to get used to the idea. I sat around for a year before charging my computer. At seventy-seven, living as a spiritual person looking back on my life in the natural world was horrifying, yet profound. I regress to the earliest remembrance of where the abuse and trauma began to present a clear picture. "Trauma is an injury to living tissue caused by an extrinsic agent. Abuse is an improper or excessive use or treatment." [Merriam-Webster Dictionary].

I recall being three years old, telling God I did not want to be here. He always responded, "Gloria, I have something for you to do. I am not letting you go until it is time." I've heard that so much I repeat along as I listen to it. I was a whining child, so says my mother, but she did not know living without God broke my heart. I whined because the thought of being separated from the Father scared me. When I could not talk, I could not tell her, but when I could, I did not think she cared. She thought I was crying for nothing and that she should give me something to cry about.

In my testimony, my life stories reveal the good, the bad, and the ugly: things that are unknown and things known but not talked about. There were hurdles I've overcome, battles I've fought, and things that still plague my life. I am not trying to impress anyone, nor do I want pity. This book is not written in pride with big fancy words to show over achievement. I wear my immaturity, ignorance, failures, disobedience, and love for God on my sleeve. The stories are true. I am withholding the names of the people involved. I lay no blame upon nor do I hold anyone accountable for any wrongdoing they have done to me. I know everyone is not in the same place with God simultaneously. I had to travel a specific path, and all that transpired had to be part of my journey. Our interactions guided me to the righteous path I tread today. It is all counted as good for my suffering that I might share an incredible testimony. I focus on Paterson, NJ, where I grew up, giving the street addresses so that people who know the city could have a more profound experience as they read this book.

The inspiration for this book is that I hope the readers will get a clearer understanding of God. It's all about Yeshua, His works, and how He can and will use people in His plan. Nothing constricts God. He is Sovereign. He does what He wants, to whomever He wants [Bible. Jer 10.6]. I was motivated to write this book to show we all must go through something. People will be free from the knowledge imparted. Some will know more of what the Lord requires of us and mature in it. I have a heart after God and a true yearning to help others set their lives on the right path. Be blessed.

March 2023

**SONSHIP: The relationship of a son to father [Merriam Webster].

**SONSHIP: is the process through which a person who does not belong to a given family is formally brought into it and made a full, legal family member with rights and responsibilities of that position. The apostle Paul used the term to illustrate the truth that believers have been given the status of "Sonship" in the heavenly family; Sons can call God, Father. Adoption makes it clear that our sonship is conferred on us, in distinction from Christ's, which is inherent. [Bible.org. Galatians 4:6]

References:

^Holy Bible Online. "Galatians 4:6. Jeremiah 10.6", KJV. Email: bibliaconsigo@gmail.com
^Bible.org. The Shaw Pocket Bible Handbook. "Sonship" Walter A. Elwell, editor. Harold Shaw Pub., Wheaton, Il. 1984. P.346.

INTRODUCTION

"In a new study recently published in the journal Memory, researchers found that people could recall things that happened to them from as far back as age 2.5 years old on average-about a year earlier than previously estimated" [verywell mind. 2021]. My memory goes beyond the new findings only because of a specific thing that happened to me. I can not put an age on it. I do not remember everything, just that I said to the Lord while still in heaven, "I do not want to go." He turned and said, "I will give you a nice mother." He then put His hand on my chest and pushed me backward aggressively. I did not feel like I was falling, but everything went black. I tried looking at case studies to help explain if someone could remember what occurred before being born on Earth. There is so much to learn about the brain, the mind, memory perception, and consciousness that I became more confused. A positive thing I read was that "Dream theorists generally agree that recurring dreams are connected to unresolved problems in the life of the dreamer" [Psychology Today. 2014]. The dreamer, that's me, needs an answer or some closure. Was this a dream, or was my brain playing tricks on me? When I asked Christ Yeshua the question He said, "You had to go. I appointed you to work for me." I left it at that and never had the dream again.

†

CHAPTER I

CHILDHOOD YEARS

I was married once and divorced. I gave birth to three sons and three daughters by two fathers. I have fourteen grandchildren, three great-grandchildren, two sisters, and a host of family members in the land of the living today. As a toddler, I recall being thrown in the air and dropping on the bed as my mother turned and walked away. I hit the bed, gasping for air, screaming at the top of my lungs when my breath returned. That was her way of shutting me up, at least for a few seconds anyway. In one of those episodes, I almost fell out of the window parallel to the bed. She caught me by my ankle, pulled me in, and shut the window. She let everyone know I was a crying child, whining all the time. That was the truth. I constantly cried. That would worry my nerves as it did hers, I'm sure.

Paterson, New Jersey, in the U.S.A., is where I was born and raised on February 25, 1946, to my now-deceased mother and father. My father was the youngest child from a family of twenty-something children, including miscarriages and stillbirths. My mother was the third child of seven children, and together, they brought five daughters into this world. I am the second child. My oldest sister is three and a half years older than me. I am eleven months older than the sister under me, and she and the younger two are each one year apart. My youngest two sisters are also deceased. I was four years old when my parents divorced. I did not know much about him except that he was a sailor in the U.S. Navy. When his tour ended, he helped a friend start a Taxi Cab Service in Paterson.

A recurring dream about my father made me lose sleep for many years.

I dreamt that my mother gave birth to her fifth child. She and my father were in the kitchen arguing pretty loudly. He was outraged. I was walking around the house in a cute little dress, whining. We lived in a building on Matlock Street, where the door from the sidewalk was the main floor. Straight ahead as you entered were huge double doors that led to the furnaces. On the left was the staircase. The first flight of stairs went up to the first landing, where my aunt lived with her four children. The next flight was the second landing, where my family lived. That day, I went into the hall and sat on the top step, listening to the loud voices. After a while, my father came running down the stairs. I had moved down to the first landing to watch the people pass by. He turned and said, go upstairs, baby.

I stood up, turned, climbed to the second landing, then sat down. I saw him enter the double doors as I looked through the poles of the railing. I sat there quietly. He was not long. On his way out he turned and saw me and said, I told you to go upstairs. I was slow-moving. He was rushing me on. When he left, through the front door, my uncle, my mother's brother, came in. He stopped and then yelled Glory, get your mother! He and their oldest sister called me Glory. He ran into the double doors and came out again. He ran past me, yelling, get out! Fire! Fire! Everyone ran down the stairs as I sat back down. My mother came and grabbed my arm and pulled me along. Standing across the street, wrapped in blankets, we watched our house and everything we owned go up in flames. We drank hot chocolate from the hands of the Salvation Army representative, too young to understand what was happening. I never knew why I had this recurring dream that would not go away. I never told anyone about it.

According to the Book of Genesis, the first thing the devil does is pull the first man created, who is the head of the household, out of place. He was not after the woman but used her to manipulate the man. God the Father made a covenant with Adam in the Garden of Eden and put him in authority to take care of the earth. He immediately fell from the position God gave him and into the position Satan had for him, which was behind the woman. Adam did what Eve told him to do instead of what God instructed. I am referencing the first two people on earth; they were created by God's hands, Adam from the dirt, and Eve from Adams' skin cells and bone fragments. Both were created in His image and likeness and had dark skin. After eating from the wrong tree, they were rushed out of the garden before they thought to eat from the other tree, which would confine them to their current condition for eternity. They were indebted to live in their wrongdoing until God made an addendum to His plan. Repentance played no part in their lives because there was no remission of sins then.

My family is generations without a father as the head of household. My mother and her oldest sister were best friends. They went everywhere together and lived in different apartments in the same building. Our first cousins were like sisters and brothers. At one point we lived with our maternal grandmother at 66 Clinton Street. She had three of her youngest children living with her. When my mother, with five children, and my aunt, with four children, moved in; people were everywhere. One of my uncles was eccentric. He saw spirits and said it was a haunted house, which made the children run through the hall screaming, fearing the ghost would catch them. We did silly things when we were young. One day, as I walked through the always-dark hallway, a man stood staring at me but did not say or do anything. I kept walking. My uncle asked me if I saw anything in the hall. I said yes, I saw a man. He said you're not afraid? I said no. I understood about ghosts or spirits as we refer to them today. I saw them myself. While it was fun because there were many children to play with, we knew our stay was not permanent. Our mothers applied for Welfare and housing. "Welfare is federally funded and state-run. They help families experiencing hardship. Recipients may qualify for help with food, housing, home energy, child care, and job training. Each state's program may be different" [USA.gov. 2023].

Because my grandma's house was too small, my mother asked one of my father's brothers, who lived at 325 Hamilton Avenue, if he could take us all in. I remember the grape vines in the backyard. He did not care if we ate grapes all day long, and we did. When my mother received the call she was waiting for, which was good news, we were all happy about having an apartment in the new housing development called Brook Sloate Development. Families with emergencies such as fires were allowed to move in early, although the work was in progress.

The single-family, two-story row housing had nothing but dirt surrounding them. There were no sidewalks, grass, or outside lights. We watched through the window as the hard workers constructed the walkways and laid the blacktop to make the finished product even more beautiful. The area was previously a graveyard. I often wondered what happened to all the bodies, but it was not that important. My sisters and I were overjoyed to move into a beautiful new apartment no one had ever lived in before. The place smelled new. We ran all around and up and down the stairs. We were proud to be the first family to live at 325-5 Ryerson Ave. I appreciate that it was called a development and not "the project." Black people are associated with and stigmatized by that phrase because the original sentiment was to gather all the blacks and put them in one place: tall buildings with many apartments. It's not that we want to live in the projects, but the real estate agencies purposefully refer people of color to specific areas, which is called *steering.

This dwelling was different. My favorite thing was the little playground because it was on our side of the development but only had two slides and a bench to sit on. Another play area was on the opposite side of the development. It had more seating, a basketball court, two sliding ponds, a shower, and swings for big and little children. I can not forget the Fire Lane. It was a shortcut for medical emergency vehicles and maintenance to have faster access to all the buildings. We rode our bikes and skates, jumped rope, played hopscotch, and played tag in the Fire Lane. An empty lot sat in the center of the development. I figured they did not know what to do with that area because it had a rocky terrain with only a little grassy area. Maintenance put up a partial fence around it. We called it the ball field. I mostly watched the games. I was not interested in stickball, softball, or baseball. I would rather play football.

Children from this area attended Public School #19 from kindergarten to the fourth grade, then were promoted to Public School #5, which started with the fifth grade to the eighth grade. Paterson was building a new school, #5, on Totowa Ave, and I was fortunate to be among the first fifth-grade students to begin classes in that building. The iconic Hinchliffe Stadium sat right behind it. My cousin formed a majorette group for the school and I was a member. It was the coolest thing to be able to skip class to rehearse in the school playground and the stadium. We practiced preparing for the parades and football games when the weather permitted.

It was a good life then, and Brook Sloate was the place to live. The residents were of mixed nationalities. There were a few racial incidents, but for the most part, we got along because we had to live there. The families on both sides of us were Caucasian; as a matter of fact, we were the only black family in our row. Our neighbors did not want their children playing with us. I thought it was more their father's commands because kids do not care about hatred. They want someone to play with. It does not bother black people until others disrespect us. I never understood why other children could not play with us and have a fun day without using the "n" word. They heard it spoken in the house and chose to use it after their parents. They had to say it at least once daily. Some people teach hate in the home at an early age. They should research to educate themselves on the origin of the word "niger." It would most likely stop the word from being used in a negative context.

Hatred and prejudice were alive and well in the fifties and sixties. In the North, black people used the front door, sat at the store counter, and even sat in the front of the bus. Still, hatred widely practiced struck hard. How could one be so bold as to tell someone else how to live? God is the one who gives life. Nowhere in His word does He refer to humans as races of people. The man gave birth to that phrase. God did not say any particular group, tribe, or family is in charge of this world. We are all beings alike and can not progress higher than the state of humanity. Some may have a grander house or make more money than others, yet they are still human. He gave the same measure of faith to each person created. The Holy One says not to think more highly of ourselves than we ought to think [Bible. Romans 12:3]. Many need to take heed of His word.

When we moved into our new place, the social worker told my mother there was a church on West Broadway if we were interested. Mom combed our hair Saturday night and tied it with a scarf before bed to keep our edges in place while we slept. We were excited to start a new life with the Lord. We took the shortcut down the Fire Lane on Sunday morning, which saved time. There was a small white building with black trim, red brick stairs, and a sign that read "Back To God's Chapel." Yes, we were at the right place. Inside was clean and filled with natural wood everywhere. A tall white woman with broad stature and dark hair appeared out of one of the rooms. We found out it was her office, and she was the pastor. We were welcomed in and asked to have a seat. We prayed, sang songs, tithed, and listened to her speak the word of God.

Eventually, the church filled up as the development filled up. My sisters and I each got a quarter to tithe every Sunday. It was a lot of money for folks who did not have anything and only received money once a month. Sometimes, my mother would give us fifty cents, one quarter for church and the other to buy candy afterward. I can still see the pastor running across the street, into the store, taking the candy out of our hands, telling us we should have put that money in church. Lord, have mercy on those pastors who try to force people to tithe or embarrass someone into tithing. Some go as far as to point their finger at a person from the pulpit, yelling, you do not tithe! *Tithing is a covenant set by God as a way to bless people [Bible. Mal 3.10]. The Israelites were held accountable for their sins through the Mosaic Law. Tithing was part of that Law. In that era, they made sacrifices for their sins that God accepted because Christ the Savior had not yet come. God sent a curse for not tithing. Today, we are not responsible for the Mosaic Law. The Living Sacrifice died on the cross, shedding His blood to wash away all sins once and for all [Bible. 1 Pe 3.18].

In these New Testament times, we are under a covenant with God, aware that our tithes of 10% and offerings of what we can give, take care of the house and the pastor. Some might say that is Old Testament teaching, but his word is forever. God also uses tithes to provide for the needs of the community. The church should have ministries that provide for the needy, and to usher them into the house of God. We are to take care of those who do not have. We should give generously. He tells us to do it freely from the heart, in love, without begrudging. When we offer, we will get back abundantly. If we do not, we will not receive [Bible. 2 Co 9.6]. I am not saying preachers fail to teach the word correctly. Some think it's okay with God to yell at and put someone on a blast from the pulpit or snatch money from someone's hand because they believe it's theirs. That is not willingly giving from the heart. You can not make people give. I heard many people say this situation is one of the reasons they do not go to church. We are not here to push people away but to draw them in. The covenant is between each individual and God. He gives us a choice to do what is right. However, there is punishment for not complying with His commands. God will send a curse our way if He wants to. There is no strong-arming involved. If there were, God would have done that already. He does not force anything. He wants us to choose to do what is right.

Summertime was our time to spend with our maternal great-grandmother at 400 Maple Ave. Wilmington, Delaware. There were twelve children in all who went to her house for summer vacation. Some slept in beds, some on the floor and the couch. My uncle slept in his car. We were everywhere. It's funny how you do not mind doing these things when you're young. Bath time was Saturday evening. We could not do that in the morning and be on time for Sunday school. I remember It was an assembly line. Three adults were involved. One helped us get in the bathtub and did the washing, One helped us out and dried us off, and the last helped us get into our night clothes.

The next day, Grandma would hum gospel hymns as she combed everyone's hair in the same style adorned with big white bows. On Communion Sunday, our clothes were all white. She would line us up single file with a switch in her hand as we walked down the side of the road with no sidewalk. People would come to the door to see her grandchildren and great-grandchildren from New Jersey. They would ask if those were her grands from up north. She proudly said, yes, they are. She directed us to say good morning. We did as we smiled and waved our hands, continuing to walk.

The church was a small one-story building. Upon entering, there were fold-up chairs to the left and the right, a pot belly stove in the front, and little room for anything else. The door was locked when all members had come in with standing room only. The praise and worship brought in the Holy Spirit, and the people went wild. The women wound up on the floor, with their skirts over their heads, screaming and yelling for Jesus. Thank God for girdles and pantyhose. I would never want to witness that scene again without them. After church, the hats sat differently on the women's heads, the hairstyles looked like they were in a windstorm, and the men all had smiles. It was pretty scary to a child.

My great-grandmother locked the door behind us when she sent us to play. The woods were across the street where we used the bathroom when she would not let us in. She saw me sitting on the curb in front of the house alone. I heard, Psst, Psst! I turned, and she beckoned me to come. At the door, she handed me a piece of candy. Eat it here, and do not tell anyone. Okay, I answered. Sometimes, she would look for me and let me use the bathroom. One day, on the way outside, she called me by my sister's name.

My sister and I were the same height. We look alike, but everyone could tell us apart. My aunt and I looked at one another and said in unison, I am not her. My grandmother went into the living room to get her switch to beat me for the times she gave me candy and let me into the house to use the bathroom. Was it my fault she did not know who she was looking at?

I should have known it was too good to be true. If no one liked me, why would she be nice to me? It seemed like I was the only one getting hit. One night in bed my cousin kept tickling me because she knew I could not keep from laughing. Grandma came in and said she would bring the switch back. I explained what was happening. She yelled, go to sleep. I do not want to hear another peep. My cousin was relentless and kept bothering me. My grandmother beat both of us but did not remove her from the bed. Still, she did not stop. I vowed never to return. I told my mother if she sent me back there, I would run away and go to the police. She laughed and told everyone. They laughed. That was the last summer vacation I spent in Delaware.

Some time later, my aunt, who lived in the same complex as us, came to visit. My mother was sitting in the chair by the phone, and my aunt curled up in the corner of the couch. My sisters were upstairs, and I was sitting on the stairs with my doll between my legs, brushing her hair. She asked her sister when was the last time she had spoken to their grandmother. My aunt had talked to her a week ago. My mother called a friend to check on their grandmother because she did not answer the phone. The neighbor returned the call. The Lord spoke to me and said, "Look up." I lifted my head and saw a still picture, which we call a *vision of my great-grandmother's living room and hall that led to the bathroom. As I sat, taking it all in, my mother and aunt conversed. The neighbor knocked on the door and windows, calling out, but there was no response. My mother suggested getting the man across the street to see if he could help. They were all friends for many years.

We waited for the woman to call back. Another call came in, and they could not find her. I said there she is, as I pointed my finger toward the floor. My mother looked at me and then at her sister while holding the phone. Where? she asked. She is lying on the floor by the bathroom, I said. My aunt asked if I could see her. I said yes. I see her whole living room. I proceeded to tell them her position and what she was wearing. They relayed the information to whoever was on the other end of the phone. I went back to combing my doll's hair. After a few minutes, my aunt asked if I still saw her. I said yes. The vision lingered until the phone rang again. Her friends looked through the crack in the bathroom blind and saw the door ajar but could not see beyond it, so they had to break in. She was in the exact position I said, right behind the bathroom door. My aunt asked again if I still saw her. I looked up and said no. My mother's face had a bewildering expression. I was about ten years old at that time. Their grandmother died of a heart attack.

When I was young, I was not afraid of the dark. At night, as I lay in bed, I would feel something circling my ankles in a figure-eight pattern. It felt like snakes the way it moved. Every time I looked under the sheet, I saw nothing. When everyone was asleep, I would sit up in bed. Most of the time, I would get up and go to the window to call Jesus, who I now call Yeshua. He would come to the window and say, "Yes, what is it?" I would tell Him again about the weird feeling at my feet, and then it would stop. I also said how I was ready to come back home and did not want to be here anymore. The name Yeshua originated from the Hebrew language and is pronounced Jesus in Greek (YouTube 2019). He was always my friend from the time of my birth. We talked and laughed and played together. He kept me company. Our apartment had a walk-in closet where my sisters and I played with toys. We did not have to clean up, we just shut the door when we finished. Yeshua sat in the closet, playing with me all the time. He would give me things to say to people around me. An adult would consider you a fresh child if you spoke when not asked, or even if you had something sensible to say, no adult wanted to hear it. I said it anyway. It was a problem with my mother when I spoke out. Keeping your mouth shut and staying in a child's place was the motto of that era, unlike today, where children speak their minds freely. I said what He told me to say.

When I was at the age to go outside to play with friends, Yeshua would ask me to say something to them. They would look at me funny. One day a girl said, she sounds like an adult, do not play with her anymore she has the cooties. I became a loner after that. No one wanted to be around me. Of course, as a child, I did not know what effect my words would have on anyone. Sometimes, Yeshua told me to pray for someone, and He did the healing work. I laid hands on people, consoled them, and rebuked devils without knowing what I was doing at an early age. I did what He told me to do. My heart broke whenever I saw a child in a wheelchair or with a cast or anyone with special needs. I would ask the Lord to heal them and burst into tears if He did not do it right then. My mother thought I was acting up and took off her shoe. Whenever He instructed me to say something to her, she became irate and punished me. A slap across the face would be her first reaction. I could quote a number if I had counted the times I was yelled at, punished, had shoes thrown at me, beaten with an ironing cord, paddle, belt, or anything else my mother could get her hands on, but I did not keep track. I did what He told me to do.

I remember, one Sunday morning, I had a good feeling. I could not explain it; it just felt good. The pastor called for those who wanted salvation to come forward. I stepped over my mother's feet to get out into the aisle. She grabbed the collar of my dress and pulled me back into the pew. Sit down, she said, and be still. The pastor was furious. From the pulpit, she told my mother to let me come up. She quoted a verse from the Bible that says, "Let the little children come to me and do not hinder them for the Kingdom of heaven belongs to such as these" [Bible. Matthew 19:14,]. My mother said no. After church, they discussed it in the office. On the way home, my aunt asked why she did not allow me to go up front. She said she's too young to understand what it means. When she gets older, she can do that on her own. I was walking behind them and heard the conversation. I said I understand it. Immediately, she turned and said shut your mouth; nobody asked you anything. When you get home, go upstairs and stay up there. I cried the rest of the way home. I went directly upstairs and sat on the side of the bed.

Yeshua said, "Gloria, stop crying, it's okay." I said through my tears, no, it's not. She would not let me go up to the pulpit? He replied, "I saved you already." When? I asked excitedly. I did not believe Him when He said that. "Watch this," He said, then lifted His right arm over my head, and I began to feel woozy, laughing out loud. I heard footsteps coming up the stairs and quickly hushed. My mother yelled when she reached the top, are you going out of your mind! She entered my room and asked again, are you going out of your mind up here? She looks under the bed and in the closet. Standing before me with her hands on her hips, she asks, who are you talking to? No one, I answered. She turned and went back downstairs, mumbling. It was apparent to me Yeshua did not speak to her. She became head deacon at church with a set of keys. She was also the person who kept the church clean. My sisters and I were her helpers. The days the different ministries used the facility totaled seven days a week. Every day, we were in the building toting our school books because she had to be there to clean up and lock up. It was noisy and most challenging when we had a lot of homework to do.

Whenever my mother was not going to be home, she left the house key in the mailbox so we could get in after school. There was a family of children that lived in the development on Angela Place across the street. They were not in school on this particular day but were outside playing. After my mother left, they reached into the mailbox for the keys, opened the door, and went inside. We thought a cyclone went through the place when we walked in from school. The refrigerator door was open. Food was all over the kitchen and dining room. Glass pieces were on the floor. In my mother's room, which was on the first floor. Perfume, powder, and everything on her dresser was all over the bed and floor. They pulled clothes off hangers onto the floor also. Footprints were everywhere.

Upstairs, the pattern was identical, but the wooden floors had ink spilled on them from the open bottles. We used ink and straight pens for penmanship in school and for homework. The medicine cabinet in the bathroom was empty, and the contents lay on the floor and in the tub. It was a nightmare. The police said this was the work of children. My mother remembered seeing them outside when she left. We found out who they were and beat them up. They were standing in the crowd watching when the police arrived. I think I was still after them about a month later. That was a hurtful feeling.

†

CHAPTER II

GOVERNMENT INFLUENCE

Being on Welfare in the fifties and sixties was tough. A caseworker came to your house to itemize your possessions. What you had is what you had to live with. You could not buy anything new. Shoes and clothes were accepted, but nothing else. They paid the monthly rent and gave us food stamps. One had to be frugal with everything to make it last until the end of the month. "Welfare began in 1932 with the great depression. The Federal Government made loans, then grants to states to pay for direct relief and work relief. Special emergency relief and public work programs were started. In 1935, under President F.D. Roosevelt's Social Security Act, the Aid to Dependent Children program was started to subsidize families that had lost an "income-producing father" [People Who Ask]. My family benefited from the program, which did not apply to everyone equally. Some people were more privileged than others, which prompted President Roosevelt to step in. He used "The New Deal" about poker and the notion that some Americans had been dealt a bad hand. Roosevelt argued that the federal government could change" [Wikipedia].

Initially, the government set the program to grant money to white people to offset their paychecks. When black people began receiving benefits, they ensured the money did not last throughout the month. They could not progress forward but stayed stagnant. I agree with President Roosevelt that what applies to one should apply to all.

My family did not have the finances to go anywhere or do anything. I wondered why our father was not with us. My sisters and I never received a letter, phone call, or anything from him; the word was he left and went to

North Carolina, where he was born. Why did he leave? Our friends' dads had jobs and brought the money home. Our family situation hurt me. I did not want anything to do with him and hated to be called by his last name since he did not want anything to do with us. His father, my paternal grandfather purchased land in North Carolina and South Carolina for his grandchildren to build on when we grew up. None of the first cousins took advantage of it, but some younger generations did.

My mother met someone after years of being alone. They had been dating for a while before my sisters and I found out. He was a gentleman and an only child. He played the saxophone in a band and worked a full-time job. His family was upset about their relationship because he was ten years younger than her, had no children, and had never been married. She had been married and divorced with five daughters. None of that phased him. He helped her by purchasing things for the house to make her life easier. We hid the new items he bought to avoid being put off the program. It never made sense to me how that could happen when no other income exists. It's just another plan to keep our people from rising.

I believe other people were so focused on how to keep pushing black people back that they could not see the future problems with this program. It needed severe tweaking. Aiding income while educating people and preparing them to leave the system to enter the work environment would have been a better approach. Program members depend on the system for too long. Workforce should have been the main goal; that is my thought. I do not think of ways to keep people from living the life God gave them. Today, we live in a perplexed world, a system that has caused dependency to trickle down to all people. Everyone, regardless of nationality, is looking for some governmental assistance.

Once my mother's friend started coming around regularly, someone told the pastor. She knocked on our door and demanded to see my mother. The same children we beat up were in front of our house. That was suspicious to me. I believe they had something to do with it. The pastor told my mother she could not have a man and have a position in the church if they were not married. She was without a man herself. How else could you get married if you do not have a man? She should have asked if they were getting married but demanded to have the keys back instead. My mother said no problem. I thought the pastor was doing her job until the argument. The Lord is not pleased with attitudes. The pastor came ready for battle. She made an unnecessary comment as she took the keys. We knew right then my mother was about to let it all hang out. When she stands at ease with her hands on her hips, she is ready to pounce. She said, go upstairs to my sisters and me. While they had words we stayed on the stairs. Nothing became of that.

I was asked what I thought about the situation. I said the pastor was right in what she was saying but wrong to come with a nasty attitude asking for the keys and wanting to fight. I should have known she was baiting me to go back and tell my mother what I said. My mother looked me up and down with pure disdain, with the corners of her mouth turned down. I was not taking sides; I was repeating what I read in the Bible and what the preacher preached. From that point on they came against me in everything I did because they misunderstood. Neither one was listening to the preacher or reading the Bible. The Holy Bible teaches us about *fornication. I Corinthians 7:2 reads, "But because of the temptation of sexual immorality let every man have his wife, and let every woman have her own husband." That is God's Law.

There was a time when the two sisters, under me and I, were all wearing the same size and sharing the same clothes. There was not much money, so there was not a lot of clothing. One sister was taller and grew the fastest. The other sister was my height. Everyone called us twins. I heard twin and short jokes, or a comment about both every day. It was the first thing people thought to do before saying hello. As we started to develop, I complained to my mother several times that nothing fit. I knew she could see for herself but said nothing. I got to the place where all I had to wear was a pair of shorts and a white shirt that was too tight. I sat on the bed one morning crying because I had nothing to wear to school. Everyone else got dressed and left for the bus. My mother said it was time to go. I answered I was not going because I had nothing to wear. She said I needed a job to buy my clothes. I babysat for a couple who had eight children while they did their weekend shopping. With the money I made, I bought a dress. I wore it so much that the kids made fun of me. To get a new wardrobe, I would have to do a lot of babysitting. I could only buy one thing at a time.

I put on my shorts, and for some reason, the zipper would not go up. I pulled and tugged and finally made it, and then it broke. I told my mother what happened. She rolled her eyes at me and shrugged her shoulders. I searched and found a big safety pin to close the front of my shorts and went outside. My shirt was worn over my shorts to partially hide the zipper. I did not care as long as they were closed. I never had friends except for one girl who lived in the development. We were the same age and in the same class. She was such a nice person. I walked over to her house that day. She was by the big playground, sitting on a bench with other teens. I heard the snickering and saw their faces as they spotted the pin. One of the boys proceeded to comment on the way I looked to shame me. He said my pants were so tight you could see the imprint of my crotch. My worry was that the pants would split at the seams, and I would not have any pants on at all, so I did not sit down.

I said he had a lot of nerve talking about somebody when he was gay. That was totally out of my character, but I was not going there with him that day. He got angry. The argument got heated. It was quiet around us as we came for each other. The others all wanted to hear what we were saying. He said something about my mother. I stood facing him with my back to the fire lane, ready to fight. He was sitting down. No one saw my mother coming. She had to have heard what he said because we were loud. She told me to go home. I ran down the lane. She spoke to the crowd, but I could not understand what she was saying. She finally bought clothes for me to wear. I'm not sure what the lesson was in that for me. I know there was not much money, but I found no reason not to buy clothes for your child, allowing her in her early teens to pop out of her clothes in public.

CHAPTER III

TROUBLED TEENAGE YEARS

Some of my mother's friends in the same housing development came over, mostly every morning after the children left for school. They would have coffee and shoot the breeze. A woman who lived with her husband and their children in the row directly behind us never came over. I got the idea early on that something must have happened between her and my mother in their youth. They would give a cold hi to each other, and then my mother would turn up the corners of her lips. My sisters and I played with her children for years. I found out my mother had a fling with the woman's husband when they were younger. I do not know what became of it.

We came home from school one day; all the windows were closed, shades pulled down, and the woman's husband was there. My sisters and I stood there looking at him. My mother said you can speak! We said hi and went upstairs to change clothes and do homework. As we went outside to play, she said do not tell anyone he is here. The following day, he was still there. We were ushered out to school and again told not to tell. A week had passed, and he was still at our home. I felt bad going to his house to wait for his daughters to walk to school every day.

One day I was asked if he was at our house. What! I said, frowning and asking if that was a question to ask a child. I asked if he was missing in action. We all laughed. Then I was asked, if he were, you would tell me, right? I offered no answer. I would have loved to have told the truth. I thought about what my mother would do to me and kept my mouth shut. I felt horrible knowing this was an adulterous affair. I was hiding the truth and trying not to let the wrong words come from my mouth. I told my mother and her friend what happened. Each time I was questioned I was ordered not to tell.

I stopped going to the house and waited with the others at the end of the row for his daughters. One morning I was sitting on a wall innocently humming when his daughter asked where I heard that song. I said what song? I shrugged my shoulders. On the way, everyone was asking where I heard it. I did not respond. She and her father created it together. It was a secret, she said. No one else knew it existed. Lunchtime came. I was determined to walk home alone, so I lagged behind until most people were gone. When I crossed the Mollyann Brook Bridge onto the corner of Chamberlain Ave and Kent Rd, his daughter stood across the street. She was watching the two sisters she was walking home with beat up a girl. The mousy white girl was in one of my classes. She was right in front of her house. She had just stepped up on the curb and stood there covering her face while the sisters punched and kicked her for no reason. They were troublemakers and fought all the time, teaming up against people.

I stayed on my side of the street to not get involved. The people in the gas station were out of their cars observing the fight. I yelled, are you adults going to watch the girl get beat up or call the police? The two heathens heard my voice from across the street. The younger one pointed her finger and said, you're next! I waved my hand and mouthed, oh, be quiet! I walked to the corner of Ryerson Ave and Chamberlain Ave to cross over. The traffic had slowed down to see the fight. No one was looking where they were going, so I could not step out. I had to wave at the cars to stop. The sister who shouted at me ran toward me when I stepped up on the curb. She hit me and ran. I went over to the girl they were abusing. I told her to keep her face covered. She was taller than me, so she walked to her door bent over. We had our hands as a shield over our faces. I said I would turn around and fight while she rang the bell. She told me her mother was working. Okay, get your key out. I will fight them while you quickly open the door and shut it as fast as possible. She did. Nonetheless, I had to fight the two heathens up Ryerson Avenue.

They kept telling the other girl to hit me because of the song incident that morning. They would push her into me, but that did not work. Although, I did feel bad. She deserved an explanation as to why I was humming her favorite song. At the end of where the single-family homes ended on that street, the development began. The first row, the first apartment, is where the double-teaming sisters lived. I walked to their door while they would hit me and run away. I would not run after them and waste my energy and strength. I called for their father, who is a pastor. He came to the door and saw his daughters in action. I told him everything and left him to deal with his children. When I got home, my siblings were on their way back to school. My mother stood beside me with hands on her hips while I explained what happened. I got to the part where they were pushing his daughter into me to start a fight. He yelled, you better not touch my daughter, or I'll!... I looked at him as he spoke. He was sitting on the stairs, pointing his finger in my direction. I turned back to my mother to see her reaction and hear what she had to say. She stood in her favorite combat position, looking at me, saying nothing, with a smirk.

He bellows the same thing at me again now that he knows my mother took his side. I responded you will do what? You are not my father! If you put your hands on me, I will have you arrested today, and you can spend the rest of your days in prison! I heard he was diagnosed with cancer and only had a very short time to live. I continued, you should be ashamed of yourself for blaming someone who was humming. You should not have sung the song with anyone but your daughter, yet you taught it to us and never said it was special. He recanted yeah, yeah, yeah while waving his hand at me. I went upstairs past him to go to the bathroom and ran back to school with no lunch.

At school, the principal's voice came over the PA System, calling me to the office. The girl I helped, her mother, and the principal were present. I spoke to her and asked if she was okay. She did not respond. Her mother asked why did you hit her and then ask if she was alright. I looked at the girl. Is that what you told your mother? I beat you up! The principal interjects you were not the one who did this? I said no. Her mother scolded her. She answered, saying the sisters threatened they would do it again. I said, and they will do it again, but I will not help you. I did not care what happened to her at that point. The principal asked what happened. I told the story and gave three names. I also said the two sisters' father is a preacher and that I told him what they had done. He calls each name over the system and then tells me to attend class. They came in the door as I was leaving. Pointing their fingers, they repeated, we're going to get you! I said oh, be quiet! I'm not afraid of either one of you. You do not want to fight. You want to hit someone that will not hit back. You hit one time and run like somebody's going to chase after you. The principal says, alright, go to class. I left.

On the way home that day, I did not see anyone. It was hot. Everyone was outside in the sun. As I walked up the hill, his wife and children were outside. His wife spotted me and began to run toward me. I cut across everyone's grass to get to my back door. The people saw she was after me and told me to run. They yelled, why is she chasing you? I was not running from her. If she touched me, she would be going to jail. The thought of calling out to my mother never entered my mind because I did not think she would come to my defense. I was trying to get in the door just a few feet away and lock it. Then she showed up. One of my sisters must have called her. They were in the backyard.

My mother ran past me and blocked this woman from touching me. I saw my mother standing at ease with her hands on her hips. The woman's head was turned aside, not wanting to look her in the face. In the living room, he is pacing back and forth. What did you do now? He says, raising his hands to the ceiling. What did I do? Go home to your wife and children, I said. We do not want you here. What are you still doing here? When my mother came in, I told her his wife was probably chasing me because every time she asked if he was here, I did not answer. I added what happened in the principal's office. Her friend left. My sisters and I were happy even though they would never admit it. I knew God was behind it, exposing it all.

One of my family members was like a spy, informing my mother of everything I said and did with a twist. I can not imagine what she told her when she snitched on me. She would start trouble and then tell. An incident occurred at the close of school one day. On the way home, my friend and I approached the crosswalk. My sister, a cousin, and a group of their friends were standing on the corner talking. Someone said there's Glo ask her. I continued to walk past them as if I did not hear it. They waved me back and asked if I would walk with my cousin to the man's house that her mother dated for years to get ten dollars. I said no. She stood there while her friends pleaded with me. My sister also stood there and said nothing. I said, one of you or all of you can go? I turned to my sister. You're her cousin, like I am. She said nothing. One of the friends said ask her yourself. She did. Where does he live? I asked. She pointed her forefinger as she said right there. There were three houses across the street. He lived in the one in the middle. Angrily, I said to them all, you are right here; any one of you could have walked with her and been home already.

My friend left. She had to get home before curfew. I told her I would catch up to her if I could, but do not wait. Let's go, I said to my cousin. I began in the direction of the house. Looking up and down the street for traffic, I noticed she had not moved. Are you coming? She stood there. As I turned to go back, she proceeded to come slowly. I asked if she still wanted to go. She nodded her head yes. We drew closer to the house. As I reached for the latch on the gate, she grabbed my hand and said I'll do it. She put her hand on the fence, leaned into it, and put her head down. Are you alright? I asked. She shook her head once again. Time was passing as we stood there, so I opened the gate and went up to the front door. She said wait, wait in a whisper. I ignored her and rang the bell. He came to the door, surprised to see me. He asked, what are you doing here? I pointed to my cousin and told him I had come with her. He did not see her at first because she was bent over behind the bush crying. He looks at me and says, what's going on? I do not know! She said you owed her ten dollars and told her to come down after school to get it. I do not owe anyone ten dollars, he said.

He waved his hand at her to enter the house. As she was going up the stairs, I was running down. I crossed the street and was up the hill before he noticed. He yelled for me to come back. I have to be home by a specific time, and I'm going to be late, I cried. He held up his foot to show me he had slippers on, telling me he would take us home. I'll wait here, I said. No! He insisted. I can not leave you out here, and I'm inside. Come on, give me a few minutes to put on my socks and shoes. I returned. As soon as I stepped over the doorsill, he slammed the door behind me. I heard a lock, then another. I turned to see seven deadbolt locks on his door as he went from one to another. I said who needs all those locks! He told me to sit down, and I answered him back, no. He picked up a sock and pretended to put it on while talking.

I was deep breathing and pacing. She was taking her time trying to get the words out. The man jumped up, still holding the same sock, thinking I was going for the door. Please, it would take me ten minutes to get out that door. My mind was racing, thinking if I should call my mother, run out of the house, or call the police on him. He would probably snatch the phone out of my hand. I sat on the edge of the chair, patting my foot. I figured as long as he would drive us, I'd make it. Just as I decided to stand up to go, he yelled at her, what do you think I am? He unlocks the door and says, get out, both of you and never come back here again! I reminded him that he said he would take us home. He said I am not taking anybody anywhere.

There was no point in running now, but I ran with all my might. I was mad at everyone. When I got home, I do not remember what my mother said or what I answered, if anything. I do remember gritting my teeth while stomping up the stairs. Later on that evening, there was a knock at the door. I believe we had just gone to bed. My mother called me. I went halfway down the stairs before I saw it was him. He looked at me and grinned like a Chester cat.

Mom asked a few questions, one being, did I go to his house, and I said yes to them. She went to get the ironing cord, took me into her bedroom, and beat me. I was hurting but knew that was coming for not asking her beforehand or getting home on time. He was sitting in the chair laughing. He accused me of something else. My mother believed it was true. I said no. He kept saying yes, it is. She grabbed me by the arm and dragged me back into the room again. That scenario played out eight times that night. Each time, he was still laughing. I did not have the privilege to share my side of the story. She believed everything he said.

I was seeing red. I gave it to him. You ought to be ashamed of yourself for lying on a child and laughing while their parents punish them. What kind of man are you? You told my mother what you thought I was thinking and doing. I never see you! How would you know anything about me? He looked like a child when he said, it's true! it's true! I told him he was a chronic liar! I then turned to her and said if you hit me one more time over what this man says, I'm going to the police. You and Aunty both say he never tells the truth. Both of them looked at me with bulging eyes as if I just revealed a hidden secret. I said I do not know what all this is about, but I will not take the beating for it. My mother says you do not know what this is about? No, and I do not care.

My mother was surprised at my response. I added, my sister is lying upstairs in the bed listening; she and her friends know what was going on, but no one told me. They were the ones begging me to go with her. I'm not her mother! I wondered if this was about her and her boyfriend in his car in the lot right in the back of their house. Her mother goes to get her. How could I be blamed for that? I turned and went to bed. The next few days, I wore turtleneck long-sleeve shirts, skirts to my ankles, and bobby socks pulled up to my knees. The welts were protruding all over my body. I could not hide the ones on my face. Everyone at school knew why I dressed like that. I acted like nothing happened and was determined not to discuss it with anyone.

A couple of days later, I walked in the front door after school; my aunt was there and said her friend had a heart attack and died. My mother was standing there with a scared look on her face as if she was in danger and apologized for what she did. My cousin told them I had nothing to do with any of it. I stood listening to all this, then went upstairs. I do not believe she would have apologized if my aunt did not prompt her. Deep in my heart, I think my aunt knew what was happening in my life. She always called me glory and knew the devil was messing with me. I vowed to God that I would never be like my mother. She called my sisters and me names and did not mind doing it. My mother cussed, smoked cigarettes, drank liquor, and would put them up to our mouths to take a puff or a sip. I would always refuse. She would laugh and shrug her shoulders. These are the reasons I vowed never to indulge in smoking, drinking, and name-calling.

I was sitting on the bed, and the thought ran through my head of how angry I was at my mother for beating me when she knew that man was a liar. The Lord appeared next to me, "You must not hate Gloria," he said. Well, I do, I said. Every time you tell me to say something to someone, they call me names, hit me, or hate me. He said, "I will take care of it all." I answered, saying, I am not repeating anything you tell me to say anymore. He said, "You are my prophet. You must be obedient." That was the first time anyone referred to me as a prophet. My mother slaps me across the face each time you tell me to say something to her. You do nothing about it. For clarity, a "Prophet utters divine revelation" {Merriam-Webster}. Utters means one who repeats what God tells them to say [Strong's 4396]. God will send His prophet to a single person or a group with a divine message.

The prophet usually will not remember what they said because the message is for the person or people to whom they are speaking.

I realized my mother did not know Yeshua like I did, but He allowed her to do those things to me. I did not want to see or talk to either of them. He insisted I be obedient. I said no again. Immediately, He stood before me, pulled my spirit out of my body, and threw it into the atmosphere. I did not feel anything. I watched it. He allowed me to see into the spiritual world as I landed in front of a big brown furry animal that rose on its hind legs to about seven feet tall and began to growl. I stood there, not knowing what would happen next, then my focus was back in my room.

The Lord had disappeared. I know that was a demon. God does send demons. He sent one to Saul in the Book of Samuel the sixteenth chapter. I felt weird as if I was without God's protection. I was fourteen years of age at the time. I was used to seeing spirits and was not afraid. My mother tried to deviate from the idea of spirits being a real thing by using a neighbor as an example. He lived directly behind us. She said when he walked around in his house, his shadow projected onto our wall. Whenever I saw a man's figure on the stairs, I ran to the window to see if it was the neighbor. I told her I knew it was not him.

✝

CHAPTER IV

FALLING INTO THE PIT

Central High School in downtown Paterson is where we went to continue our education. In my teen years, I had friends all over the city. I heard a couple of boys from downtown liked me. I shrugged it off because I was not into them. Whenever young folk got together, they talked about sex and relationships. That would be my cue to leave. A friend asked why I did that. I am not interested, I said. She said you have to talk about it at some point. No, that was not for me. I enjoyed dancing and being her friend. She was a member of St. Luke's Baptist Church of Paterson, on Carroll St. I was invited to go with her family every Sunday because she could not understand how I could sit under a white preacher. I did not see any difference. Preachers are all supposed to be teaching the same thing. I went with her family occasionally and slowly veered away from my church. School dances are what excited me. I love to dance. I won contests at teen hops, which were teen dances back in my day.

Things started to change for me. One thing after another happened; nothing positive, nothing good. Evil began to raise its head. My life became a downward spiral. With every situation I went through, I thought of the incident with the Lord in my room. He had not spoken to me or answered when I called. I know I was being punished. Some Christians believe God allows us to live our lives the way we want and that he will judge us on the last day. The Bible says we should live our lives through Him. He judges and keeps notes on everything we do and say daily. The end is the final judgment {Matthew 25:31-46}.

My mother's youngest sister is the same age as my oldest sister. We call her by her first name, not Auntie. She lived with her mother in Delaware and was taking a train to Jersey to spend the summer with family. Since the high school was close to the station, she came by to get my house keys. We talked for a few minutes as I waited for someone to open the door that locked behind me when I came out. A guy came down the street, stopped where we were standing, bent down, and smiled in my face. I jumped away from him, and he went on. She asked do you know him? Never saw him before in my life, I said with a foul look on my face. I asked if she knew him. She answered no. In my mind, he looked like the demon I saw in the spirit.

Some boys from downtown began to hang around at Brook Sloate. I stayed inside to avoid listening to their immature babble. They would come to our house when my mother was at work, attempting to enter through the windows and the front door. We called the police, but by the time they showed up, the boys would run. The phone rang one afternoon. My mother answered and called me to pick up the extension upstairs. It was a boy wanting me to come outside. I told him I did not want to talk to him and slammed the phone down. He called back. She answered. I slammed it down again. After several times, I told him this is not my phone; please stop playing on it. My mother shouts well, you should not have given him the number. I yelled back with an attitude. I did not give the number out. I called my friend to see if she knew who did. She mentioned another friend of ours. I confronted her about giving my number without asking me first. She said he kept asking her over and over. I said you should have told me. We became enemies from then on.

The first high school dance I attended was with one of my sisters and her boyfriend. He was quiet and had a car with green lights underneath that lit up the street at night. I was supposed to go with them and come back with them. It was late when the dance was over, and everyone was hurrying to get out of the building. When I reached the car, it was full of teens who lived in our area. There was no room for me. They squeezed together and sat on each other's lap. I stood on the street with the rear door open, telling them to make room for me. Suddenly, someone approached me from behind, trying to pull my clothes off. I turned around, and it was the same guy who grinned in my face—the same guy who called my house.

We were scuffling by the open door, and I fell backward into the car on top of everyone's feet and him on top of me. I put the palm of my left hand under his chin, pushing his head backward and punching him with my right hand. I was yelling help me. No one did. I flipped on my side, and he somehow slipped and fell. I slammed the door and locked it. All these people were in the car, and no one helped. Neither person in the front seat said anything or even turned around. If the shoe were on the other foot, no one would do that to anyone with me there. The person would have been in the hospital or jail. I was devastated and embarrassed.

My heart was pounding. I rode all the way home on the floor of the car with people's feet on me and in my face. He stopped by the fire lane to let everyone out. I ran into the house crying and went upstairs, vowing never to go again. I hated going to school because I did not know if he was in school or just hung around there. Someone said he was a student my sister's age and was addicted to drugs. I did not know anything about narcotics, but I believe it because he looked older.

I ran for the bus each day to keep him from spotting me. I had to run into the police department once because he was chasing me. The police station was a corner building on Ellison and Washington Streets. I entered on Washington Street, and the door slammed behind me. A tall white man in a suit jacket and jeans said, what are you doing here? Out of breath, I pointed and said, I'm trying to get to the bus to go home from school, and this guy is chasing me. Get out of here, he yelled. He picked me up by the neck of my coat, opened the door, and threw me to the ground.

My right hip hit the meter post, but I got up quickly, thinking the guy was probably watching. I saw my bus pull up at City Hall and ran to catch it in time. I was shaking, holding back my tears. How do you go to the police for help, and no one helps? Upon arriving home, I told my mother what happened. I told her he chases me all the time. She laughed and said puppy love. What is that? I asked with my eyes wide open, and my face frowned up. She puts her hands on her hips and says, oh, Gloria! I ran upstairs crying. Many thoughts were in my head, trying to figure out how to avoid him because she would not help. How often do you have to tell someone you do not like them? I called on the Lord, but He said or did nothing. When you reject Him, He rejects you. We went from talking all the time to not speaking at all.

A friend of one of my sisters lived on Angela Place in the development.

She never stayed at our house but came only to get my sister to go to her house. On the school bus, she would have something to say. Everyone heard her but did not know she was talking about me. She never mentioned my name. It was always about something that happened in our house. There was nothing funny about what she was doing, telling everyone our business. She must have thought I was afraid because I never said anything. I rolled my eyes and shook my head. That went on for a while.

The day came when I was not taking it anymore. We boarded the bus and took a seat in the back. She started her nonsense before we were underway. I immediately cut her off, which stunned everyone on the bus. I let them all know she was talking to me all this time, and I was not taking it anymore. She and I went back and forth while I enlightened others about what was happening. The people could not believe she had the gall to comment on our household that did not involve her.

Whenever I entered the house, my sister and mother would look at me, whispering and snickering like two schoolgirls. I stood looking back at them, wondering what kind of family this was. I stood up to the friend and did not back down, giving her word for word, comment for comment. She became frustrated on the bus one day and must have wanted to fight because she said she was going to get her sister to beat me up after school. She probably thought I was too young for her to hit. I said do not count on it. The girl she referred to is a friend not her sister. We all lived in the same development. I said that she should mind her own business. I am not afraid of you or her.

The next day, the girl she called sister approached me at school, asking me what my problem was. I kept walking as if I did not hear her, then turned around and went back. Her older sister was there leaning against the fence, listening. Their mother, my mother, and my aunt grew up together. I knew them well. I put my finger up and said no! Mind your own business. Stay out of it. You and I will get into something that will break up our friendship. I told her I was surprised she would interfere like that. She laughed and turned away. I was glad about that. She and I had no problem with each other, but I was shocked she was okay with interjecting herself into our dispute. People do what they do regardless of who gets hurt. At school was where I continued to be harassed. I tried to ignore it as much as possible. I could not figure out what was happening and why they were against me. Trouble was stalking me and I wanted to know how to get off this downward spiral.

Somehow, my mother's caseworker was alerted about her relationship. I believe it was the mother of those children who told on her because we, mostly me, kept beating them up. We were put off the program and had to pay a higher rent. My mother found a job working at night. Her friend moved in to save money and probably to keep the boys away. I took the blame for that, but it was not all me. The boys were coming to see one of my other sisters also. She did not mind opening the door to let the boy she liked into the house. When she did the other boys would bum rush the door. I was tired of being blamed for everything that happened and truly hated my life.

My mother's friend was a great person. His perception of me based on the twisted stories he's heard could not be good. Christmas was happy and fun with him around. He did not mind spending his money to make my sisters and me happy. He took us out to dinner once a month, on Garret Mountain to play, and always at Guernsey Crest and Gelotti's, the places to go for ice cream. They were his favorites. I felt terrible because he was not my father. I felt like someone was spending his hard-earned money on me and should not have.

When I was fifteen, we moved to 190 Governor Street on the Eastside. It was a gray two-family house close to the corner of Carroll St. My aunt, and her family took the first floor, and we were on the second. I was sad about the move because I loved Central High and Brook Sloate. Unfortunately, we left the west side, moved to the east side, and now we will be students at Eastside High School in Paterson, NJ.

One of my cousins was a football player at Central High. He and the other players started a club and wanted to make money to hold different activities. He asked his mother if they could use the basement to give a social. That is what we called a house party and charged a fee to get in. She spoke to my mother. They had to think about it long and hard. There would be teens everywhere, loud music, drinking, smoking, and drugs. They were not up for that but thought one time would not hurt; they could make some of the money back they spent moving. The word went out with stipulations from our parents. There will be none of those things going on.

Anyone who smokes has to go in the backyard, and any fighting will shut the party down immediately.

On the day of the party, every teen from the north, south, west, and east side of Paterson showed up. My cousin was the DJ set up in the basement. That's where the dancing took place. That's where you could find me. Everyone could not fit in the basement, so my mother made the overflow come into the yard instead of standing in front of the house. People were in and out to get air and purchase chips and soda our parents were selling in the backyard. Someone kept turning the light off downstairs. It was pitch black, and the music was loud. My mother came in cussing, turning the lights back on. You do not want to mess with her.

An uncle, a cousin, and the football team were chaperones also, but it seemed like she did the hard work. When the party was over, no one wanted to leave. It was the funniest thing. My mother kept saying it was time to go. They would move a little. It's time to go! They moved a little more. After clearing everyone from the basement to the yard and from the yard to the front, they had to get them to move from in front of the house. She raised her voice, saying, you do not have to go home, but you have to move from here; good night! At the end of the day, it was not too bad.

In school, everyone raved about the party and asked when the next one would take place. Oh no, our mothers do not want to hear that. They told us what they disliked, and we relayed it to our friends. They wanted a party, so they agreed to do whatever was necessary. The next party was on. Our mothers went shopping for snacks and drinks. The kids came in droves. We were popular before the parties, and it showed, especially with all the football players in attendance that topped it off. The money made was too sweet not to have another and another and another. We had socials every weekend.

The day before Easter, a friend and I were trying to decide whether to go to church or the movie. The movie won out. She figured the churches would be overcrowded, with people thinking that attending church one day out of the year meant something. Then we decided not to go anywhere. On Easter morning, April 22, 1962, I slept in. Everyone was milling around with nothing to do. I got up for a little while, then went back to bed. It was a dull day from the start. My sister entered the room and said many people were gathering outside and I should come and see. I was not interested. She returned and repeated the same thing: You should come and see. The crowd got bigger, they said they came to go to the movie with you. With me! I got up.

My jaw dropped as I looked up and down the street, filled with people. Yes, we knew them, but I only spoke to one person about going anywhere. I leaned into the window and asked what was going on. They said they had come to go to the movie with me. I responded I am not going anywhere, so go and enjoy the rest of your day. I turned and went back to where I was. It was getting to be late afternoon, and I could not believe those people were still waiting for me. I said okay, let me get dressed and see what's going on. I thought about going with the group to get them away from the house. They are lucky no one called the police.

When I went outside, I saw a friend I met through my younger sister. We became close. Her boyfriend and the guy who tried to rape me were sitting on the wall in front of my neighbor's house. They were best friends. I asked her what was going on as we started walking toward downtown. She said, ask him, pointing to the would-be rapist. I looked at him and rolled my eyes. I said I'm confused. We turned down a street off the path. I asked why we were going this way. The guy says we have to pick up a friend. I said aren't there enough friends? When we arrived, he was getting ready, so some people went inside to sit and wait. Before long, everyone had gone in except me and my friend. Her boyfriend came running out, grabbed her by the arm, and pulled her inside. I followed them in.

We went through the small kitchen into the empty living room. I turned to ask where everybody had gone. The boyfriend pulled her through a door, slammed it shut, and locked it. I traced my steps back to where I came in, and the lights went off. The rapist entered the room. He said no one is here but us. I asked, what is going on? He answered, you said the only way you would go anywhere with me was if we were in the same crowd of people. That's not what I said! Some time back, he asked if he could take me out. I said no; the only way I would go anywhere with him was if we happened to be with the same group of people at the same time. I certainly did not mean as a couple.

So you set this up! I was livid. I thought what could he have said to all those people to make them gather like that and wait in front of my house? Did they know what he planned to do? I went to walk toward the door when he grabbed my arm. I smacked his hand and yelled get off me! We began to wrestle. He was a football player. I believe he joined the team because they were always at our house. He picked me up, threw me on the bed, and climbed over me. I was kicking, squirming, and screaming. I heard fighting in the next room, and then it stopped. I screamed Jesus! Jesus! He raised his fist to punch me. I grabbed his fist and turned on my left side. He held my hands down by putting them under his knees. That did not benefit me because I was so tired I could not move. He won over and raped me.

It was dark in the house, and I did not know how to get out. He showed me the way to go. I ran screaming and crying the whole way. It was dark out. People were looking at me as if I were insane. I could not remember where I was, but through my tears, I found my way. I ran into the house crying. I went straight to the bathroom to bathe, rubbing my skin hard to erase what just happened. I was in a daze. How could this be happening? I told my mother he raped me. She did not believe me. She thought I was out there having sex all along. There was no surprised look on her face or hurt, Or empathy. I do not remember her comment, but it broke my spirit. My heart fell to my feet. My knees went weak, and I almost collapsed to the floor. The pain I felt because of my mother's lack of love and unbelief was astronomical. If you can not turn to your parents, who can you turn to? Where is my father? I am without support from either one of them, or from God. What is going on?

I felt weird going to school, knowing everyone knew what had happened to me. The girls carried hardcover black and white notebooks. They would write a name on it and then ask everyone to write something about that person. His name was in the books. I thought they were waiting for me to express myself in those books. Several times, I said I would not do that but changed my mind. One girl kept pushing it at me. I snatched it and wrote; I hate him! He is a rapist! Die! Die! Drop dead! I figured everyone would get the picture. She asked why I would write that in her book. I said because you kept shoving it in my face. As I walked away, they were saying let me see. What did she write? Shortly after that, I found out I was pregnant.

I went into a deep depression. I took my time as I walked alone. I moved around like a zombie, not concerned about going to school. My friend was always on my side. I told her what the doctor said. The others found out when they saw it in full bloom. She told me that day she and her boyfriend got into a fight in the next room because she was trying to get back to where I was to help me. She was dark-skinned, but the bruises were there. She had a black eye. I thanked her but did not expect her to get beat up. Where was everyone else? I asked. She said they went in the front door and straight through the back door, which led to the street around the corner. I had no hatred toward anyone but him. I just felt like my life did not matter. Nobody cared.

His mother wanted to meet me. I refused to meet and greet any of his family. We were not a couple, but they were my child's family, so I agreed. He was high on some drugs when he came to get me. If his older brother was not driving, I would not have gone. His brother visited his girlfriend, and we visited their mother's apartment in the Alabama Ave Projects. He knocked on the door a couple of times. No one answered. I questioned if we were at the right door. He used the side of his hand to pound on the door. I said obviously, she's not home. He backhanded me across my face, and my head hit the brick wall. I stood there deep breathing with my hands on my head. He hit me again. I began screaming at him to keep his filthy hands off me. He yelled shut up! I said you do not tell me what to do. I found myself lying on the floor face down. I was six months pregnant at the time.

From the floor, I looked up at the window. There was a large jar of Vaseline sitting on the ledge. As I reached for it, I looked over my shoulder to see he was nodding, almost about to fall over. I put my hands around the jar and slammed it on the window sill. The whole bottom came off and left a jagged edge. He came running at me. I thought to stick it right in his face and pull it down. He lifted his head, and I cut his throat by turning my hands in a circular motion. He felt the blood running. You cut me he said in amazement. He ran down the staircase. I sat down on the sill, waiting for the police. I just knew they were coming. I thought I'd rather be in jail than be with him. I found it ironic that the whole time I was in the hall, no one opened their door, came out of the elevator, or came up the stairs. I sat there all night. No one knew where I was.

The following morning, the elevator opened. My sister walked out. We were looking for you, she said. Why are you still here? I was waiting for the police. She said there was no call to them. We walked to her boyfriend's car. He picked him up from the hospital. They were friends, and he was in the back seat with a wide bandage around his neck. I got in, giving thanks for the ride. The rapist told me that he ran to the Barnert Hospital, which was not too far away. The doctor said one-sixteenth of an inch more, and he would not have made it. I said I would not have done it if I cared if you made it or not. He said you should at least be sorry. I responded, sorry? I am sorry I had to cut your throat. I meant to rip your face off! My sister and her boyfriend gasped at my comment. You will not beat me down. I let him know I was going to stand up for myself.

A few months went by. Someone in the rapist's family was having a party at the Audubon in NYC and insisted I go. I hardly felt like dancing, having fun, or even moving as big as I was. I certainly had nothing to wear. I wore a pink lace dress that everyone thought was a short dress. If they only knew I had the waistline pulled up over my belly because I could not pull it down. The night was long and loud. I was tired of sitting in that chair and was ready to go. It was about midnight, and I had not seen him the whole time we were there. I went looking for him, and found him in the stairwell with a bunch of females. He was heavy in the act of having sex with one of them. The others looked like they were waiting in line for their turn. I looked around at them all, then yelled, I'm ready to go whenever you finish. I turned and went back inside. Back at the table, his mother asked if I found him. When I told her what he was doing, she asked, Why would you look for him? I do not give a care what he's doing, I said. I'm ready to go. She sent his brother out there after him. She was not happy about the situation. You see to it she gets home, she told him.

He must have taken something before we left. On our way to the Port Authority, he stops and sits on the ground. I said what are you doing? I forgot which way we were supposed to be going. As teens, we slipped off to New York to the Audubon to dance now and then. I looked around. Nothing is familiar. Okay, get up; let's keep moving, I said. He's bobbin and leaning along the way. He says let me go in here for a minute. He wanted to pee in an alley. I waited too long and decided to follow him. He was asleep in the back of the building on the ground. Oh, are you kidding me? I shouted. Drugs make you sleepy! I could not wake him up enough to be coherent, so I waited in the dark until he got enough sleep. I was furious and tired of standing, jumping at every sound I heard. His eyes opened. He looked around and then looked at me. I was leaning against the wall with a big belly in a pink lace party dress, with my arms across my chest and a scowl on my face.

He stood up, brushing himself off. I thought of how everyone else was home already. I watched the new day dawn through the darkness then asked him to direct me toward the bus station. I was ready to go. He laughed. What's funny! Is this the way you treat somebody and think it's alright? Let's get to the Port Authority now, or I will find a police officer. He reaches for my hand as if I wanted to hold his nasty hand. I jerked away and kept walking. We were not far from the station, but we were going in the opposite direction. Tears came to my eyes when the bus pulled in. I waited until he paid, then said I will not sit next to you. He went to the back of the bus. His mother must have given him money, or maybe someone else did; I do not know, I just wanted to get home.

✝

CHAPTER V

TRAUMA AND DRAMA

Life on Governor Street for my family was short-lived. My mother and her friend separated. I would be the last to know the circumstances. She started dating someone she knew before. He was moving to Pennsylvania with his mother and asked her to come. She went there to look for a job and a place to live for her and my sisters. She said I could not go because I was pregnant. Then where will I go? I asked. Find somewhere, she said. What does that mean when I am sixteen and pregnant with no job?

She asked her sister, who moved to an apartment on North Second Street If I could stay there. She said no. She told my mother that's your daughter, take her with you. Next, she asked my grandmother, who lived on North Third Street in a one-bedroom apartment with three other people. Her response was there was no room. Where would she sleep? My mother said she would be back to get me after the baby was born. My grandmother took me in.

December 1962, I gave birth to a 7 lb baby girl. After the baby came, I slept at my grandmother's kitchen table with my head resting on my arm. My daughter was in the carriage in front of me. I could not stay there, so my aunt took me in until my mother could think of something. My aunt talked with me right away to find out what feelings I had for the father of my baby. I told her I had no feelings for him except hate. She said that can not be true. He raped me! I kept saying I do not know him or like him, but no one believed me. He does not appeal to me; most importantly, he is a drug addict. I have no feelings for him at all. The next thing she said shocked my socks off. Then I hope you do not mind if I see him. I stood

— 35 —

there. What! I thought about it for a second. Unbelievable! I do not care, but really!

Life meant nothing to me. I did not want to live let alone take care of a baby, with the way my mother was trying to shove me on other people. She was trying to think of everything but take me with her. That first night at my aunt's house, after I finished cleaning the kitchen, bathing the baby, and feeding her, I sat down in the corner of the couch where I slept sitting up. I burped her and laid her down in the carriage to sleep. Around nine o'clock that night, my aunt unlocked the living room door and entered her bedroom. A few minutes later, he came in the door and locked it behind him. He leaned over as if to kiss me. I slapped his face and told him to drop dead. I watched as he went into her bedroom. At six in the morning, he left to go about his day until nine at night when he returned. That was their routine. When we were having the socials, I remember there was talk about my cousin walking in on his mother and somebody having sex. There was an argument, and he put him out. I never found out who that person was. I wondered if this was the continuation of that episode.

My mother came to Paterson to talk me into getting married. No! I said. The baby has to have the father's name, she said, and where would you live? He is the one that's supposed to take care of you, not me. Where are you going to get money to take care of the baby? She kept hitting me with questions, which made me question myself about what I would do. I said I have to think about it. Where does he work? Does he have a job? She went on and on. She suggested we all get together with his parents to discuss the problem. He lived with his father on North Third St. I went to speak to him, and he came to the meeting.

He and his wife were divorced, and both remarried. He was the owner of a construction company and said I can do nothing. I can not take you in because I have all boys and there is no room. He said his son has a job with him as long as he comes to work. He suggested to his son that it was time to put on his big boy pants and take care of the family he had created. I was not his family, but that was his baby. He told him to look for an apartment immediately. He was a very nice man, laid back with an even tone in his voice. My aunt added she could ask the preacher on the corner to come to the house. I lifted my head and looked at her with a frown as if to say what are you doing? My mother said okay, that's a plan. My mother set a date. It had to take place before she went back to Pa. I stood there thinking she could not wait to get rid of me. What kind of mother is this? What is going on?

For my wedding, my mother and aunt made snacks and drinks while I sat on the couch staring. I wore the same pink lace party dress. It fits a little better now that I lost the weight. I only had three or four things to wear; that dress was my formal attire. The pastor came, then the perpetrator and his father. The proceedings started. I was not listening until the preacher asked if I would take this person to be my husband. Wait! What! That was the first time the pastor heard me speak. He repeated the question. I stood there thinking, not saying anything. He announced that he needed to talk to me in private. We went into my aunt's bedroom. He shut the door behind us, which did not improve the situation. He explained his position. He could not move forward if I disagreed with this marriage.

Anxiety took over, my head was pounding from the thoughts racing through it. No, I am not in agreement, I thought, but where would I go? What would I do? How would I feed my baby? I should not be on the street with her. I asked if he knew of somewhere I could go. He offered a simple no. I was disappointed. Churches should have resources to help people with any problem they are facing. My mother was set against taking me. I was not staying with my aunt and her nonsense. I thought to myself, I'm sure his father would help. I wiped the tears that were running down my face and said yes. He knew I was lying. You want to tell me about it? He said. I shook my head. Not if you can't help me. I need a place to stay. We went back and finished the ceremony.

My husband found a furnished apartment on Cliff Street off North Third Street. His father most likely gave him the money. It was an old wooden house with paint peeling off every plank that squeaked when you walked up the stairs. I believe it was leaning to the left a little. We were on the second floor. Moving in was easy. All I had was a few items in a shopping bag and baby stuff. He took us there and then left to go to the store for something to eat. I cleaned the stove, refrigerator, and table while he was gone. The furnishings were old but still functional. He returned with raw chicken, potatoes, seasoning, and other items. I laughed. I do not know how to cook chicken. He said you're going to learn. No, I'm not, I said. I do not cook. He said he invited his father to our first dinner. I could not stop laughing. He left. I cleaned the chicken as much as I knew how, then peeled the potatoes. I decided to make mashed potatoes and fried chicken.

A knock came at the door. It was my new father-in-law. I opened the door and said, I must warn you I do not cook. He said, oh no! Then I'll have to tell you what to do. With that being said, dinner was a disaster. I thought I did everything he told me. I had high hopes. The potatoes were okay. You could eat around the lumps, but the chicken was pink inside. We sat at the table, ate potatoes, and talked for a while. I explained my situation and how I got to this point. However, I did not expose the relationship that was going on with my aunt. He apologized for his son's actions. He told me his wife cheated on him and became pregnant then said it was his. When the baby was born, he looked like his biological father and nothing like him. He put his wife out but kept the baby. They kept this information from the child. As he got older, he found out that the man he thought was his biological father was not him at all. He began to act out and turned to drugs. Yes, my baby's father had serious issues. I thought my issues were over the top. My visitor left and I began to clean up. My husband came in, but I did not ask where he'd been. I figured he was at my aunt's house carrying on. Was my dad here? He asked, looking in the fridge. Yes. Did you feed him? No, the meat was raw.

The baby was sleeping in the carriage in the living room. He looks at her and then pulls me into the bedroom. No! No! I said. I was not having it. We began the struggle. I noticed as he tried to get me on the bed he looked out of the window. The Riverview Towers Housing Project was directly in our view. He acted as if he knew someone was watching. I asked who are you looking at? I reached to pull down the shade. I was ready for battle. I screamed, "What do you think I am? He turns and runs out the door. The next day, his father came by to tell me he went to jail on a drug-related charge. I called my mother. She had to pick me up because I could not afford the apartment.

In the meantime, there were issues in Pa. My sister fell, broke her ankle, and was on crutches. The man my mother moved in with was a woman abuser. I heard they did nothing but argue and fight. The day she picked me up, she had bruises. She told me right away I had to get a job. When we got there, all my sisters rushed to see their niece. They took me upstairs to show me where to put everything. The bedrooms were huge. It was an old house with a cold burning stove. That's the way they built them years ago. You would want to keep the fire lit. When it died out the house would freeze over. We took turns. Whoever was in charge of the fire had to get up and restart it.

There was loud arguing in the bedroom downstairs. I went down and sat on the couch next to my sister, who was sitting on the floor trying to keep cool. She said she had an operation because her ankle bone ripped through her skin when she fell. Inside the cast was hot. It itched so bad she was using a knitting needle to scratch her leg. My mother's bedroom was off of the kitchen. I tip-toed to the hall to see if I could see anything. My sister waved me back. I was trying to see what he looked like. They all acted as if nothing was going on. The argument got heated. I heard thumping and ran to the kitchen. My mother saw me and shouted get out of here! I shook my head and said, No. I stood there. She screamed at me to go back to the other room. He turned his head to look at me. I looked in the drawers to find a knife and held it as I stared back. He walked past me and out the door, leaving her on the floor. I put the knife back and went to the living room.

His mother prepared dinner for us because she wanted to meet me. I said I will not! When the time came, they left after asking me repeatedly to go. She lived across the courtyard. There is nothing like sending him home to Mama right across the street. They kept sending someone to coax me, so I finally went. I watched and wondered why they were eager to go, but the older woman was a lovely person who spoiled her only son. I guess she felt bad for my mother. It was a blessing when my sister told me she would be willing to babysit. She would be home since she was in a cast. That was music to my ears. Before I could get a job, my baby's daddy was back in our lives. My mother said I had to go. Back to square one again. How do you get help if no one is willing to help? I need a babysitter to get a job.

After a short while my mother was planning to move back to Jersey. She reunited with the last man. He had joined the Paterson Police Department before she left. He must have cared for her to take her back. They made plans to get married and buy a house. 497 East 18th Street, Paterson, New Jersey, was the new residence for my family, three houses from the 11th Avenue intersection. It was a nice area that was changing fast. There were a few black families that lived on the block, but the majority were white people who began to move out quickly. On the 11th Ave corner sat the phone booth I used to call my mother and ask for help. She gave me an emphatic no! I asked who put their daughter and baby out in the street without helping them or at least providing information on how to get started. She said alright, you ask his parents to help, and then we will help. Your husband is not my father. I am not his responsibility. She hung up. I slept on the floor of the phone booth that night.

The next day, I asked my baby's father if he thought his family would help. He went up to see his mother. She told him to go to the office of the project where she lived and apply for an apartment before she let me stay there. I am glad she did that. His mother did not like me much although she knew nothing about me. I assumed that from the sneer on her face when she looked me up and down. She spoke to me as if I was some peasant. There was plenty of work for me to do. I did not mind the work, but after I finished, I was too afraid to move around because of the judgment I suffered. I sat in the corner of the couch with my daughter on my lap, talking to her and teaching her. His mother made comments about me holding my daughter and not letting her loose to play. One of the comments she made constantly to her family and friends was that I do nothing but hold that baby. That statement was not true. How was the work getting done? I could not hold her while sweeping and mopping the floors, making the beds, or washing the dishes. Why does everyone treat me wrong, and no one says anything about him? Anyway, I was thankful. I was not outside and was ready to do whatever she asked.

✝

CHAPTER VI

THE TRIALS OF MOTHERHOOD

The apartment came through. Right away, my husband went to jail again and was not able to move in. I signed up for welfare because I was jobless. My mother gave me the twin beds my sisters had when we were young. They were in my bedroom, and the baby's crib in her room. My stepfather would pick us up to go food shopping and do laundry at their house. I never bought furniture, and it was a good thing. After six months, my husband was released and the welfare department cut me off immediately. They said he had to take care of us. It was about four days before he came to the apartment. Someone told me he was staying with two sisters who lived on the same floor as I did.

On a sunny afternoon I had the shades pulled up. The baby and I had a morning of playing. I fed and bathed her and put her down for a nap. Looking through the living room window on my way to the kitchen, I saw him standing there with the two women, looking back at me. They are the sisters I fought with in Brook Sloate Development. He comes through the door, trying to start something with me. They were looking through the window, so I closed them and pulled the shades. He grabbed me by the wrist, and we struggled into the bedroom. We fought through the whole thing. When I got my hands on something to hit him with, he was out the door. I wanted him dead. I was tired of fighting. I was tired of him touching me.

I moved one of the beds into the baby's room and stayed there while he slept in the other room whenever he came in, which was not often. He stayed mainly down the hall by the sisters. It was like pulling teeth trying to get milk and baby food from him, but he thought he could come in and abuse me anytime he felt like it. He would get up each day like he was going to work with his father. When I saw his father, he said his son came to work maybe once or twice and never returned. I was furious! How was he paying for the apartment? His father did not know, nor did I. When rent time came, I asked for the money. He always assured me he was going to pay for it. I watched as he went into the office each time. There was never a notice or complaint from the office. I thought he was doing his job.

There was a knock at the door. I was shocked to see the Constable standing before me and even more shocked to hear what he had to say. You have to leave now; I will wait. I froze. I was stunned and could not think of anything, not even my name. He said you should be packing. Why? I said. The rent is not paid, he told me. But I saw him go into the office. He said there was another door on the other side. He probably went straight through. I was quiet, then said, but no one sent notices. He said, your husband most likely got to them before you did. Is there someone you can call? No, I answered, shaking my head. If I were you, I would only take what is necessary. I shook my head yes and thanked him.

Since I was walking, I needed her carriage. I packed her clothes, pampers, food, and bottles. I had just finished making formula and filled the bottles, which were still hot from sterilization. I wheeled the carriage into the hall and then went to get her. I grabbed a couple of outfits for myself and put everything between her and the bottles. When we stepped over the doorsill, the man put a padlock on the door and left. I thanked him for waiting and stood there with my daughter in my arms, wondering what to do and where to go. We went down on the elevator, sauntered past the neighbors, and strolled down Market Street. The thought came to me that I am again with no place to sleep. I was on the street with a baby, but the abuser had a place to lay his head. I had to make some serious decisions. I had nowhere to go except my mother's house.

As we approached the train tracks on Fair and E.18th Streets, the carriage wheel got stuck in a big hole surrounding the track and tipped over. I caught the baby. Everything else fell out. I carried the carriage to the sidewalk, put her in it, and picked up all the items except the jar of milk that shattered and spilled. My mother was not home when I got there. I let her know my plan when she came in. She was not happy to see me. She was upset I only had the things in the carriage. It's a good thing I had a carriage, I said. I could not carry a crib or bed. I had to leave immediately. She yells at me why didn't you make him pay the rent? I paused, then said, like you made our father take care of us! For as long as I could remember, she had to fight every man she was with. Is that what is going down through the generations? Why me? I called the next day to see if I could get the rest of my belongings from the apartment. They told me to pay what I owed. I was broke..

The human predator dared to ring the doorbell, looking for us. I answered the door. You are not welcome here, satan. Do not come here again. You ruin someone else's life and leave me alone. I had all I could take of you. I slammed the door and started a life without him. Divorce from him was one of the many sighs of relief in my life. I decided to keep his last name. I was not taking my father's name back; it was a trade-off for me. The Welfare Department had to restore my case when I explained that he was living with two women, and I was locked out. Shortly after, at the doctor's office, I found out I was pregnant. My stomach churned when he told me. He asked if I was faint. I guess the look on my face told the story. The way I felt I could have killed myself at that moment. I had to come back to reality because there was already a life I was responsible for, and now I have two. September 1964 was the birth of my daughter at 7 lbs 3 oz. Years later, I heard their father killed someone and died in prison from an overdose.

One of my mother's childhood friends used to manage the Elks majorettes. One of my sisters and I marched with them; I quit after getting pregnant. She asked if we would march because there were not enough girls. Although I loved being a majorette and marching in parades; I was not feeling it after having two children. I told her this would be the last time. We found our boots and short skirts and headed to her house. It was exercise, and I needed that. The parade ended at the Elks Club on Broadway in Paterson. They were going to have a celebration, but I was not staying. I had to shower and wash my hair from sweating under that heavy hat. My sister was leaving with me.

We handed in our headgear and left. A guy was following the parade, asking for my name and number the whole time. As my sister and I left through the front door of the club, he was double parked in a gold convertible car waiting for us to come out. Where are you going? I will take you. Do you take no for an answer? I asked. I am not looking for anyone in my life. The answer is no! Stop bothering me! He said I'll take you home anyway. He kept following us. About halfway home, we got in, and he dropped us off. My hair was in tangles from the hat; it was a mess. He asked if he could come back to pick me up. I said no, I have two children, and I cannot go anywhere. I thanked him for the ride. Later, when my daughters and I were sitting on the porch, he drove by, turned around, and came back. He probably did not realize it was me when he passed the first time. I looked different. I washed and straightened my hair out, which was pretty long, and had on long pants with a white ruffled blouse. We talked for a little while, and then he left. He had a thin, muscular build and a fair complexion. I do not like light-skinned guys because they think they are God's gift to the world. He was full of himself, and I told him I was not a fan.

He came over one day to see if I would take a ride to talk. I was not inviting him in so I went outside. My sister said she would watch the kids. We drove around the city, discussing a relationship I did not want and why. I wore a thin trench coat and slippers on my feet. I asked to go home because we were expecting a snowstorm. He said no and pulled over to talk some more. It was a game with him. He would not start the car, so I opened the door to get out and walk. He said he would take me home. On the way, he parked in front of a house and said, I want to introduce you to someone. It will just take a minute. I went inside and met his mother and siblings. He was showing off, and I was getting weird vibes. An argument ensued between him and his siblings. The dispute got heated and turned left. The things they were saying to each other were horrible. It was time to go. The hints I gave were in vain, so I said aloud, when are we leaving? He answered I'm not moving the car; it's snowing.

Oh no! I jumped up. I forgot all about the storm, I said. The windows had drapes that were closed. His brother pulled back one, which allowed me to see how hard the snow was falling. I ran to the window. It had accumulated on the ground. I asked in anger, how am I going to get home? He shrugged his shoulders. I said you should have taken me back where you picked me up. I asked his brother for my coat. He said you can not walk with those shoes on. They told me I could stay. I recanted, I have two children; I could not stay then I asked to use the phone. I called to tell my sister I would come as soon as possible. I had planned to wait until the plow came through and walk in the street. His mother told me I could lie in his bed since the plow had not come yet. He and his brother had bunk beds. I laid down across the bed with my clothes on, and he sat in the chair that was in the room with his head against the wall. I call myself listening for the plow but do not remember hearing a thing.

When I woke up the following day, my underwear and pants were down. He was lying next to me. I was furious. I yelled, You did this! You do not know what you did is rape? You fool! I hate you! He kept apologizing over and over. His mother looked sorrowful but said nothing, not that I recall. I wondered what she was thinking. The city finally plowed the streets. He took me to my front door. I could not get out of the car fast enough. I told my sister what happened, excluding the rape. He kept calling and apologizing. When I had a few minutes to sit down and think, I wondered what life was all about. What is going on? Why me? It can not be just me. Are girls going through this like I am and not saying anything? What is the matter with guys that they feel they need to rape someone? Why do they think it's okay? They have no control over their bodily functions. My solution to their problem is castration. I am dumbfounded for the third time. I am pregnant. This guy's mother had the nerve to call me a baby breeder. Your son is a rapist, lady. The seed of life is in the loins of man {Hebrews 5}. Girls are the ones who are blamed and put to shame. Someone needs to teach boys to keep their hands to themselves.

I felt something was forcing me into a way of life, and I did not want to go. But what does it all mean? Where is God taking me? I thought that must be what was missing, so I went back to church. There was always something about church that did not sit well with me. The one I frequented, I called an upscale one. It was close to home, and we did not need a ride. In my opinion, it was where the middle class went, who thought they were the rich people in town. The prideful strutted in with their suits and ties, gowns and furs, grinning and waving. They only spoke to those who looked like them. Honestly, there was more socializing than worshiping. It was a circus. I was frowned upon, but everyone loved my daughters and knew their names. I had a purpose for being there and did not care what people thought of me. My life was at stake. I needed answers.

I gave birth to a son, my third child, in July 1966. My daughter started preschool in the Head Start Program. We waited a long time for a spot in our area, and we had to walk from the east side to downtown every day. The school bus transportation was not available, and I had no money. She would ignore you as you spoke to her, roll her eyes at you, and things of that sort. She would not pick up after herself to save her life. We walked to school and home again every day. It was hard for me because it was four times a day. Her teacher said she was so bright she did not need Head Start. She could go right into second grade. Enrolling her In a higher grade would be out of her standard age group of peers. I did not want that. I asked the teacher about activities they did in class because she got so she refused to walk home after school. Every day was becoming a problem.

We would hang around the building, sitting on the grass for a while, then start our journey uphill. I tried to take the quickest route. Halfway home she would lay down on the ground protesting the long walk. Her usual protest for anything was to lay down on her back, cross her ankles, and place her hands across her belly. The people who passed by looked to me for answers as they walked around her. She would stiffen her body if anyone tried to get her up. I would let her lay there for a few minutes. Time was of the essence. I had to get the others. Carrying her on my back the rest of the way was how I did it until I could not do it any longer.

My grandmother was moving out of her apartment on Marshall Street. It was an attic apartment on the third floor. She said she would ask the landlord if I could rent it. He agreed. She moved out. I moved in. There were problems from the start. The building was full of roaches. My apartment had no second way out. I had to go down to the second-floor apartment to use their back door to take out the trash. The backyard was small, full of trash bags and stray cats. No one went back there. A huge hot water tank sat in the kitchen. I had to light it with a match every time I needed hot water. It got really hot. When the water was heated I turned it off. Once I forgot to turn it off and went to my mother's house to do laundry. The neighbor downstairs called to say I left the heater on and it was overflowing. My stepfather rushed me back to turn it off and clean up the mess. I was not used to this at all. The heater was indeed a challenge with three small children. The baby kept climbing out of the crib and I was afraid one day the tank would be lit.

My son's father was seeing a girl who had the same name as my mother. She lived the next street over from me on Main Street. Since I was up on the third floor I could see his car parked whenever he was over there. I would have to call out his name from the window, which embarrassed him in front of everyone when they looked up. I only called him to do what he was supposed to do; pampers and milk. One day he came to see what I wanted. Are you kidding me? I said with an attitude. I called you for the same reason I always do. He was angry and did not want to go to the store. He stood at the foot of the staircase when he returned and threw each item up one at a time telling me not to call him again. He threw the milk so hard it put a hole in the wall. Milk splattered everywhere. I hurried to pull it out and found an empty jar to salvage what was left. I yelled at him, you get angry because you have to spend money so that your baby can live? He said you get welfare. No! Your son does not qualify. I will have to sign you up for child support and they will come after you. No white man is going to tell me what to do, he said. That would be his mindset. It's all about him. He thinks he is having it hard when I am the one trying to survive with three young children. You are the father of this baby and you have to take care of him. No one should have to tell you that. He came back the next day with milk and the materials to fix the wall, apologizing again.

My daughter started Kindergarten right across the street at School #3. It was a pleasure to be able to watch her walk down to the corner to the crossing guard when I could not leave the other two alone. If they were still asleep I would walk with her. That apartment would have been the ideal place for that reason but I knew we were not staying there long. I could only open one window. Between the roaches, the heater, and cats walking on the roof looking in my windows; I could not do it anymore. I stayed until my lease was up. My mother and stepfather's tenant would be moving in a couple of months. They said I could have the apartment. My son's father helped me lay something down to get rid of roaches in the new apartment before we got there, and then I sprayed the furniture before we loaded it in the truck to leave most of the bugs where I found them. Goodbye, good riddance. That was an experience I could not wait to get away from. My mother suggested we set off bombs at the same time on all floors to run them out of the house entirely. We did. My ex kept asking if he could move in. That was not my plan. I said, no, you have a girlfriend; I am not playing those games.

He was a mechanic at a car dealership in Wayne, NJ, and loved his job. He came to my house every day after work to see his son. I guess that was his way of ensuring me he was not involved with anyone. He was a very finicky eater and I did not know how to cook. I fixed what the kids liked, that was easy for me. His mother lived up the street, and if he wanted to eat here every day, he had to supply what he ate. He started taking me to the market every weekend and paid for anything over the amount I had in my pocket. I do not get it. Men love to have sex but do not want to comply with the consequences that come along with it. If taking care of children is not in their plans they should do something to prevent it.

Men are the ones with the seed, but they leave that for the women to do. The first thing the devil did was pull the man down from where God placed him. Our men need to get back in position. Whenever I mentioned church, the bible, or God he would run out the door. Being with him was like having another child who was reluctant to listen to anything I said. Why did I keep taking him back? The changes he made in his life did not change his sex habits. He would come in from work, shower, and hit the street. He came back in the wee hours of the morning when I would be asleep, and would wake up with my clothes off. One day I felt funny and could not explain the feeling. I said I better not be pregnant.

That same day after the kids were in bed, he brought a guy and his dog to the house with him. I asked what are you doing with this dog in my apartment? Sir get this dog out of here! My son's father says this is for you. I looked at him as if he had two heads. What is for me? You do not want to be pregnant, he can help. So what's the dog's job? The guy says, do you want this or not? Listen here, do not talk down to me in my house. First of all, I should have been asked instead of just bringing it to my face. I am not sure if I am pregnant. I just commented. He says, well this will let you know. I let him insert a tube in me then the three of them left.

I woke up the following day with the tube lying on the bed. I washed it and set it aside to give it back. Two days later I saw light spots of blood. I figured it was from the tube. Later that evening, I went to the emergency room because when I went back to the bathroom, there were spots in the commode. I explained to the doctor what happened. He asked if I saw anything in the toilet. I said no. There was no more blood and I was not in pain. He suggested I have a DNC. The doctor explained what that entailed, and said the procedure took six to eight weeks for recovery. After the procedure, I lay in the hospital bed wondering if I I had to go through this procedure? I was just trying to make sure I was not pregnant. As soon as the six weeks ended, I woke up in bed with my clothes down to my knees. Not again! I screamed. Look, are you insane! This is rape! How many times do I have to tell you? I could have you put in jail. It does not matter if we are a couple and have children together, you are doing it without my consent. I was in total agony. I was done. Get out! I yelled. I had to get away from him. August 1967 is when my fourth child, an 8 lb 3 oz baby boy was born.

The postpartum depression this time was more profound than any other. It was not just my head and heart that were affected. I could feel it in the pit of my stomach. I felt as if I was in someone else's body, looking through their eye sockets and being controlled by them. I could say I did not care about anything but I did care about the lives I brought into this world. Someone had to take care of them. I kept telling myself it had to be me. I decided I would not just get my tubes tied, but to have them cut. My doctor said he would not do it because I was young.

That is the excuse he gave me. What kind of doctor are you? I already have four children. I made appointments with the Gynecologists in the area to see who would do the work. One was a black doctor that just about every black woman in town frequented at that time. They all turned me down including him. Either they could not take on new patients or they were a little leary of why I wanted to change doctors. I thought of just walking away from it all like the men do, but it was not something I would do. Men would not give a second thought about walking away from their families. I could not figure out for the life of me, why the fathers think that way. I ended up with deadbeats.

My sons' father was the type of person who harasses you until he gets what he wants. He begs over and over again, like a spoiled brat who can't get their way. He was relentless, never letting up. We had a conversation about his selfish childish tactics. He said his mother told him any woman would want to take care of him. My head turned toward him with fire in my eyes. You should have told me that in the beginning. I assume she said that because girls like the way you look. She is dead wrong. My preference is not a light-skinned man who focuses on himself and thinks he is finer than everyone on the planet. I prefer someone who respects me and is willing to do what he is supposed to do. Did she tell you the man is the one who provides for and protects his family? That comes from above, not your mother. She can not turn it around. These children are your seed and you are supposed to take care of them.

I reported to my case worker that I had another child on the way and she said we have to add them on. I would receive a little more food stamps but not money. She said the father had to pay through the system. I assume they think he gives me money that they can't regulate. He was not a happy camper when I explained what had to be done. I'm not going to let a white man tell me how to live, he said angrily. I said, your head is hard. You do not want to listen to anyone telling you how to live. Just when I finally get him to the place where he paid for some of the groceries this happens.

Christmastime was his season. He spent money and spread good cheer. The spending bug hit him hard and I utilized that time to get what our children needed. We argued that he wanted to fill the house with toys and I wanted to get clothes and shoes. We compromised on two toys each and the rest would be clothes. After the court proceedings he stopped everything. The amount the court ordered him to pay was so little it couldn't pay for dinner but he was determined he was not going to do what the white man said. It never crossed his mind that money was to purchase shoes and food for his children. He persuaded the woman who did payroll on his job not to take the money out of his weekly paycheck. The system immediately took it out of my monthly check.

My situation went downhill like a sled on an icy path to nowhere. I was confused. I was getting assistance for my two daughters. Welfare could not add money for the boys to my check, which paid the rent, but took money out for what my sons' father was supposed to pay. This action put me in a place where I did not have the total rent at the beginning of the month. They could have left the boys off like I wanted and insisted the job send the money. What kind of system is this and who is it supposed to help? When I find a job I would be working just to pay for the sitter. Truthfully, I need two jobs to cover everything. There was no one I knew who would watch them for nothing. I was desperate and began harassing him the way he did me. I went to his job and acted a fool because they were not sending the few dollars allotted to me. That is a court order! I commanded, standing in the middle of the floor with my finger pointing at the ceiling. He did not like being embarrassed; still, nothing happened.

I took a computer course, then entered the work program, and suffered through that period in my life because I had to get this done. I was always after him looking for money to pay a sitter or leave them by themselves. A call came in one day, late in the afternoon, from a man with a nasty tone in his voice. I give you fifteen minutes to get down here! I held the phone for a few seconds then said, you have the wrong number and hung up. He called again and said, Get down here now! I asked who was playing on the phone. He said you just get down here. Where is here? I asked. He said, the welfare department for your six-month recertification. Well, you could have just said that from the beginning. I need a babysitter, so I can not come today, I could come tomorrow. You get down here now, he said. You have fifteen minutes. I need more time than that because I have children to get ready. We have to walk. I do not have a car or bus fare. I'll see you tomorrow. He said that I would be cut off by then. I hung up. After I thought about it I said let me see if my mother would watch them. She did not want to. She wanted to know how long I would be gone before committing herself. I figured about an hour or an hour and a half. I gave the baby a bottle, changed him, and put him to sleep while the others went downstairs.

It took me twenty minutes to run downtown. I entered the building and sat down as I looked around. Police officers were agents then. There was only one person with no one in his chair. He was shuffling papers going back and forth to the printer. He sat down giving me the side eye with the corners of his mouth turned down. I stood and asked loudly if he was the one who called me down here. He said, I do not know, you didn't give me your name when you came in. Well, I said, I can tell by the sound of your voice you are the one because you did not give me your name when you called. He had a shameful look on his face. I gave him my name. He motioned with his hand to come. I got in his face and yelled, never call my house like that again! I do not care who you are, your gun and badge do not scare me one bit. If you do not know how to be respectful, let someone else call. I did not run down here to watch you sneer at me and shuffle papers.

The Sergeant came out of his office. He asked," What is going on here?" I told him what transpired. I ran down here from the east side and left my children with someone who did not want to watch them. I have to run back because I have no bus fare. He looked at the officer with surprise, then took my paperwork, and we went into his office. I told him I had to go to the car dealership because they were not sending the money. He said we do not chase after the fathers. Really? Well maybe you should. There needs to be a new system, I said. Then he said he would give them a call to see if it helps. I thanked him, signed the papers, and left.

When I came, my mother, stepfather, and a few of their friends were sitting in their living room. My daughter was putting on a show. She had no idea I was standing there. She proceeded to stick her tongue out at the adults, hold her five fingers up to her nose, moving back and forth making sure all of them got it. The other children were playing a game on the dining room floor. I walked up slowly as she turned to stick her butt out for them to kiss. She froze. Puzzled, I stood there with my arms folded across my chest not saying a word. I looked around at everyone who remained quiet. I asked if any of them had ever seen her do this before. No one answered so I asked again. They said no. I was wondering what brought that on. Where did you get that from, who did you see doing that? I asked. She stood there. I took her by her shoulders and turned her around to face them, apologizing to everyone for her behavior. She would not apologize. These people are adults, not children your age. She still would not apologize. I told her if she did not apologize she would get a beating.

After a few more times of asking she still would not say anything. The others put the game back and went upstairs while she lay down on the floor in her usual posture. I grabbed her arm and slid her out the door and shut it behind us. Standing over her in the hall I said, get up off the floor now. I tried picking her up but she was twisting and turning. I could not get a hold of her. I said I am not going to fight with you, get up! I started up the stairs and let her lay there. She began to whine as if she did not want me to leave her. I turned to go back down and she hurried to lay down again. I turned and went up calling her to come upstairs. You are going to get it. I stormed back down and pulled and carried her. I knew she was doing that because she was in trouble. She was over the top and acted up.

I grabbed her, took her to the window, and said I should throw you out.

I let go of her, let her fall to the floor and left her there crying. I told the others not to open the door. Leave her out there until she finishes crying. When the noise stopped I opened the door and asked if she was ready to come inside. She said yes. I asked a couple of times why she was acting like that downstairs. She just stood there looking at me. I said okay I'm not playing with you anymore. I got the belt and sent her to her room. Since then she has been telling people I tried to kill her. Really! If that was the case she would not be here today. Before I left, after I put the baby to sleep, I took her into the living room, sat her down on the couch, and explained that I had to run downtown to sign papers. She wanted to go outside. No! I won't be long. You can go out when I get back. If you are not good you will not go outside. I told my mother she could not go outside until I got back. She knew not to act up but did it anyway.

Just then there was a knock at the kitchen door. There stood my mother in her attack pose, feet spread, hands on hips, and lips curled up. I just looked at her until she spoke. I whipped her ass! What! The thought went through my head, aha! She repeated as she shook her head, I whipped her ass! For what? I asked. She wanted to go outside. I told her no. She kept asking so I told her to stay on the porch. When I went out there she was not there. I called and called. She was in the neighbor's house. I turned to look in the bedroom at my child. So you got hit twice for not doing what you were told. Now I know why you wouldn't tell me what happened. You did not listen. My mother says so what do you want to do about it? I said, What? She repeats it while still standing in the hall. I said, oh please, waving my hand at her. I knew something had to happen to her, I just could not figure out what it might be, then I shut the door.

I looked up and said to the Lord, I do not know what her problem is. She has been edging me on trying to get me to fight her for years. I am not going to fight my mother. It's hard, though, to ignore her when she's looking for a fight. But why? She has been slapping me across the face since I was little. I turn and walk away each time. You see it and do nothing. I did not know if she was listening at the door, but I was more angry at Him than her. What use is it for me to come to you about a problem and you do nothing? Why should I try to do what the Bible says when it backfires on me? You always tell me to be a bigger person. He said, "Look at what they did to me. I went through it." I quickly interjected You volunteered for that. You were willing. I am not willing to let people beat me down and stand there and take it anymore. I am tired of it. If I had enough money, I would not live in this house or this city.

A couple of my sisters were not doing any better than I was. My mother did not want me to leave because then she would have to give the apartment to one of my sisters. One thought she should have it. The other was laid back and did not care if she got it or not. I was truly grateful to them for letting me have the apartment but it came with ungodly stipulations because I was the daughter my mother could not tolerate.

My ex was back in the picture. He said he would help if he could move in. Although I could only put up with him for a short time I allowed it. It was not the right thing to do but I was desperate. He is supposed to take care of his children no matter where he lives or who he lives with. I took the bargain for a short time because I needed help. My fifth child, my third son, weighed 9 lbs 10 oz born in August of 1969 on the same month and day as my last child. He was a breech baby. It is unbelievable the things the doctor had to do to turn him around. He was born with a peaceful look on his face, sucking his thumb as if he was smiling at all that just happened. It was because I did all the work. In the end, everything turned out okay.

I remember about six months before giving birth to him one of my sisters came upstairs and said the family was gathering downstairs. She had come to tell me they were talking about my son's father, saying he was a troublemaker and was running from the police. She said my stepfather, who was an officer, and his partner were chasing him but did not catch him. They said the arrest couldn't take place because of me. I was unaware that any of this was going on. I was furious at them all. I told her I had nothing to do with it. Tell them to do their job. Look at the situation, I said. Here I am, two and a half children later, and the family has been whispering behind my back about this but no one said anything to me. This is the type of gossiping, backbiting turncoat family we have. The fact that my stepfather was chasing him and we were living in his house bothered me a lot.

I confronted my children's father when he came in. How dare you! I said. You live in this man's house knowing he is the officer that's been chasing you. You look in his face like you are untouchable and said nothing to me! I can not deal with you. You have to go! Get out now! The usual gathering place for family was my mother's house, except for me. I would go downstairs to say hello to everyone, make my children go outside then I would come back upstairs and turn my fan on exhaust. Smoke rises. The smoke filled my apartment when everyone came over. I did not drink, cuss, smoke, or gossip and I was not going to sit down there in it. Family members did not understand my reasoning and said I thought I was better than them and shunned me. I do not care what they think this is my life.

I noticed the arguments My mother and stepfather were having sounded like they had money problems. No one that lives in the other house they owned was paying rent. My stepfather came upstairs with an attitude demanding we stop using so much water. He said let the kids take a bath once a week. I felt I was being harassed again but did not argue with him. After not bathing the kids for a week. I decided I was not going to keep doing that. Playing hard had them smelly and dirty. I washed them in the sink and sent them to school all week like that. I told my stepfather to give me the water bill to pay. I did not know how I would do it without borrowing from the rent so I began looking for a part-time job that would pay me under the table. My son's father went to his mother who was the cleaning lady for a doctor she had been with for a long time. He asked his mother to see if the doctor needed help in the office. I took that job but it was only when one of his girls was out sick or on vacation. However, the money helped pay the expense which was due every three months and the rent was paid on time.

My brain hurt continually worrying about how to borrow from Peter to pay Paul; trying to figure out how to keep a roof over our heads; how to take care of the children's needs; and pay the bills with little money. Numerous times I did not eat so there would be food for everyone else. I wore the same clothes for many years because I couldn't afford new ones. My shoes were glued together and polished to hide the wear. My children never knew the hardships. I did not want to saddle them with negativity and problems of poverty at their age. How could I tell them they could do anything if they were weighted down with the reality of what it took for us to survive in this world? I used to be able to hear things while sleeping and immediately wake up. Aging, and the nonsense life threw at me wore me down. Giving birth and raising children made me feel good and tired. When I lay down now I go to sleep immediately. Nothing disturbs me anymore. During the time my children were growing up I slept until my brain said okay I had enough. Every time I woke up it was on time to do something for the kids. My life indeed was not my own.

My youngest son did not go to preschool like the others. I kept him home and taught him myself. There was no sitter or program at the time. It worked out fine because he is an introvert, very shy and quiet. My other children said they thought he could not talk until he was ten years old. He spoke to me all the time. Teaching him gave me something to do to keep my mind off of why and how. I was at a place where I was just getting through the day, trying to keep a straight face when I wanted to break down and cry. Everything was building up inside. I encouraged myself by saying it won't always be like this. I had to keep pushing through for them. My son was three years old when I gave birth to a daughter weighing in at 11 lbs 11 oz in January 1973. God commanded us to be fruitful and multiply; which means have sex and reproduce. If nothing else worked in my life that passage did.

This pregnancy was the result of a booty call. One more time my son's father tried to convince me he matured and wanted to get married. That will never happen! You are stuck in the player syndrome and not even looking for a way out. This last pregnancy was complicated. Everything that could go wrong did. It was not easy to get around. I had a hard time breathing. My feet swelled up so I could not wear shoes. I ate crushed ice all day every day. When I could not find it I bought the cubes and crushed them myself. Something went wrong with my right hip as the fetus grew. I did not know if she was lying on a nerve or what, but the doctor claimed he couldn't find anything wrong. I had to deal with the pain and discomfort. I was miserable. My ex moved in to help because I could not do a lot of things, ecstatic he was having a daughter this time. He was a twin. His sister was stillborn at birth. The doctor said I could be having twins. I prayed daily for the opposite of that diagnosis to come to pass.

My delivery date was the seventeenth but manifested two days earlier. The night of the thirteenth I heard my mother come in and I thought I would go help the kids get to bed because it was late. I offered previously to help the kids with their homework every day and make sure they got to bed on time while she was at the store. My mother declined with a salty no each time I suggested it. This particular night her best friend was with them. My mother put her hands on her hips when she saw me. I stood in the doorway offering my help and did not notice the friend circling to the back of me. She grabbed me by the wrist. I turned to see what she was doing and my mother ran up and began slapping me in the face. I stepped forward to hit her back and her friend grabbed the other arm. She was holding them behind me while I was being assaulted. I yelled get your hands off me. I'm calling the police to have you both arrested.

They quickly moved away from me. I slammed the door shut and went upstairs. The one day that I had enough of her slapping me and was willing to engage in a fight I couldn't. My blood was boiling. I could not calm down. I paced back and forth trying to decide if I wanted to put my mother in jail. As I reached for the phone I felt in my spirit that was not the thing to do. I knew that was God. He and I disagreed over Matthew 5:38-40. I am fine with giving something away if someone asks for it, but turning the other cheek after they already hit me once, I am not doing that. I could never understand why He wanted me to allow someone to do whatever they wanted to me; yet I could not defend myself. I know the verse mentions an evil person but God means any person. Still, in a huffy attitude, I said to Him, do not say anything to me. I am in a fighting mood and if she comes up those stairs it's on. He insisted I get a hold of myself. I knew my actions warranted punishment and it did come. People think God is so loving and kind that He will not punish anyone. God is faithful to His word and His plan. He will exude love and punish us at the same time. He does not dwell in anger and commands us to do the same [Psalms 37:8].

The next morning my stomach was feeling shaky which lasted most of the day. I went to the hospital that night when I felt pain and was told my labor had started. While I waited I instructed my children on what needed to be done while I was in the hospital keeping to myself what transpired some hours before. When the time did come my doctor was nowhere to be found. I lay in the delivery room waiting for them to find a replacement doctor. I could not for the life of me try to describe the labor pain so I will move on. When the fill-in doctor entered the room the Anesthesiologist had me by my left arm as I was hanging half off the table screaming at the top of my lungs. A nurse came in to tell me to lower my voice. I was scaring the other mothers who were waiting to deliver. I know I said some things to her that I do not recall and she ran out of the room. I believe Satan might have taken over and said something to her at that point.

The Anesthesiologist had tears streaming down his face. He straightened my body on the table and rubbed my arm and shoulder because I was not feeling any effects from the drugs. No doctor, no medication, I could have stayed home. The doctor arrived and stood along the furthest wall watching until it was over, not mumbling one word. I do not believe he let the drug specialist go through that trauma alone. The only time he moved was to sew me up at the end. I was hoarse but remember saying I wanted to have my tubes cut because I could not go through this again. He shook his head yes. Suddenly the medication went flowing through my body. That is all I remember. I almost did not make it through this childbirth. Each one of my babies was larger than the last. I noted their weight each time so you can see the progression. I shudder when I think what the next size would have been.

I slept until the next day. The Anesthesiologist was the first person to visit. He was a very compassionate young man and was worried about how I was doing. As I thanked him. The nurse came in to take my vitals and told me how much the baby weighed. I started crying. I had an idea the doctor knew I was having one baby and told me it could be two. It was too big and he did nothing about it. I believe that's why he did not show up for delivery. When I went to his office for a checkup, hurting or limping, he and his assistant behind the desk made comments about me coming in like that, when every woman in the office was going through the same thing. On one occasion a tall white woman, who was minding my business said, that's right, we are all pregnant. I asked her if she was my height, or was her baby as big as mine. Do you have pain in your lower right side? Are your feet swollen so you can't wear shoes? She answered no to everything. Then everyone is not going through the same thing as I am, I stated. The doctor was prejudiced. My mother used him for her pregnancies. That is how I started with him and we did not get along. The things that came out of his mouth were unacceptable. This is the same one that would not do the procedure of tying my tubes.

While at the hospital, something went wrong with my blood pressure so I could not see the baby. I was informed that I had to get a CAT scan. They saw something but no one knew what it was. A team of doctors came rushing into the room and put a rubber mat under me. They said they had to go back inside of me. The Anesthesiologist moved aside as I began to cry, Oh my goodness no! With all the stitches I had I was scared. They kept apologizing, I kept screaming. They pulled something out that shook like jello and looked like a calf's liver but larger, that's how I explain it. Three times he went in. Three times he pulled the same thing out. I never saw those doctors before and never found out what that was. My doctor had prescribed iron shots for me every day because I was anemic; So he said. I figured I probably didn't need it and it had nowhere to go. Whatever it was could have been mistaken for another baby, but it did not have a heartbeat. On top of what was happening to me, a nurse picked my daughter up by her arm and pulled it out of the socket. They laid her on her stomach and tied her arm to the bar of the crib so that when she moved it would pull back in place. It worked. She stayed in the hospital a couple of days longer than I did.

It hurt me to sit, stand, lay down, walk, and even talk for six months straight. I cried and moaned the whole time. I would not wish that pain on my worst enemy. My mother came up to get the baby and take care of her until I was able. I had to be carried to the bathroom by my elbows; I bent my forearms up, placed them in my ex's hands, and held myself stiff. He lifted and carried me. He stood me on the toilet seat to use it, put me in the tub to rinse and dry, and then brought me back into the bedroom. It's a good thing he was strong and didn't mind doing it all. I could only lay on my back which was painful. He took care of me and the children. They complained all he fed them was beans and hot dogs and vowed they would never eat them again. They were glad to see me back on my feet. Thank you, Lord!

One of my sisters lived down the street on my block and another around the corner. They both had children who loved to spend the night at my house with their cousins. I let them do that on the weekends. I would cook a big breakfast on Saturdays and Sundays for them. Most were boys. They played games, watched TV, talked, and laughed. They doubled up in the beds and did not want to leave. The phone began to ring at ungodly times of the night. I jumped right up so the phone would not wake the kids. When I picked up no one answered. I heard breathing so I asked who it was, and they hung up.

Once someone said, bitch! I was too through. I recognized the voice even though she tried to disguise herself. It was my sister who lived down the street. I called her name to let her know I knew it was her. She hung up. She was a street runner, drank alcohol, took drugs, and every man she met she gave them my name, address, and phone number instead of her own. I did not know these people. I changed my number so many times until the light went on. I never gave my information to her. My mother was the emergency person for the school or anything else. Every time I changed my number I gave it to her. She gave it to my sister. How does your family think doing this is funny?

Family was gathering at my mother's house once again and I had just finished cleaning when the same sister came upstairs. She stepped over the door sill and my eyes stayed glued to the glass in her hand. I held my hand up to stop her from going any further. I was leery of her intentions and wondered what she was up to. She wanted to confess. She told me she and my children's father had been hanging out together. What that meant exactly, I did not think to ask at that time. She knew I do not allow liquor in my house so I was aware something was up. She let a few tears fall and apologized. That is what actors do. I told her to get out of my house with her nonsense and slammed the door in her face. My first thought was to push her backward out of the door and down the stairs but I left her in the dark hallway instead.

On the way home he had to stop to pick up a three-piece dark brown corduroy suit he had tailor-made. When the door opened I was standing there red hot. I snatched the box, threw it on the floor, and wiped my feet all over his suit. I tried to rip it to shreds but couldn't. So, you two think you're slick, I said. I watch the kids all weekend while the two of you party. You lay there when she calls at three in the morning and you say nothing. He quickly grabs his outfit off the floor and runs down the stairs and out the door. I guess he saw the word kill in my eyes. Now her mission was accomplished. She got him out of the house but she got her kids back. No more sleepovers.

†

CHAPTER VII

WITH GOD IN IT

My son started kindergarten. He loved seeing the new faces but wasn't fully adjusted to the new lifestyle. I used to walk him over to the school to watch the children in the playground to prepare him to get out of the house every day. We talked about his teacher and classmates he would have. When the time came he tried to cling to me. He cried for a couple of days. It didn't take long to adjust. Waiting outside the door as he came out gave him confidence that I was not going to leave him. By the time he went to first grade, he was accustomed to school.

I received a call from Calvary Baptist Church Daycare one block from the house and I registered my two-year-old toddler. I had been trying for years to get my children in that daycare and now they had an opening. My oldest daughter dropped her off before school and picked her up every day after school. Everyone is out of the house at one time so I can start something new. I took a business class, a computer class that consisted of keypunching holes in cards, and an office management class. I enrolled in William Paterson College in Wayne, New Jersey. Psychology and Child Psychology were my majors and Mathematics was my minor. My goal was to work as a psychologist with the school system when I acquired a degree.

Going to school during the day hours worked out fine. The night classes were the problem. My mother switched to the midnight shift on her job which she loved. She went to bed at four in the afternoon and school let out at three twenty. While I was home I could keep my children on a schedule that would allow her to get some sleep. I wrote out a plan and hung it in the kitchen so they could follow and learn the routine. They loved to play, run, and jump, so I knew there had to be noise over her head. It was the thing that was constantly on my mind. I survived college for two and a half years pushing it as far as I could. I was trying to get as much under my belt as I could so when I applied for a job I could make a good salary. To live required money and I was penniless. My bills were not getting paid on time and the children were acting up in school. Because I had to go to school full time I couldn't work or spend much time with them. I had to study and do homework just like they did.

Not eating was part of my lifestyle. My body adjusted and it no longer affected me. One Friday evening there was nothing for dinner. I asked each one of my children if anyone had a quarter or any change at all. I was trying to muster up enough coins to buy a loaf of bread so they could at least put something in their stomachs. They didn't have anything. We went to bed that night without eating. I was not too concerned because they did have breakfast and lunch. The next day I cleaned the house to keep busy. I let my family know I would borrow money from someone to get food. Then they went outside to play. I had no one I could ask for money. It was Saturday and by noon I was in tears and mad at God. I opened all the cabinets and the refrigerator door. There was absolutely nothing in the fridge but light, which was so bright I thought the Lord came down from heaven. I stood back and told Him to look in and tell me what He saw. I said I am tired of crying and begging for food. These are supposed to be your children. You gave them to me to take care of. You are the one who supplies all our needs and you have yet to do that. He did not say a word. One hour later my son ran upstairs telling me my stepfather had a lot of food in his car and wanted me to come take some.

The Paterson Police Department started a summer program at the Masonic Temple on Broadway for the youth whose parents were incarcerated. They wanted to give the children somewhere to go and something to do during summer vacation. No one showed up. My stepfather said he drove around to get the word out and tell the children to come. They packed the car with food, drinks, games, and toys to hand out as they went. The couple of children they talked to were not interested and did not want to take anything. The officers collectively suggested my stepfather take the food so it would not go bad since he had so many grandchildren. That was so nice of them.

Our kitchen was overloaded. Everyday there were drinks, hot and cold cereal, buns, fresh fruit, salad, sandwiches and more. We supplied the neighborhood children and others outside the area that played with my children, with food daily for the entire summer. The officers did not want to shut the program down in the hopes that someone would show up next year. But no one came again. The program had to close. Games, balls, and toys were donated to hospitals, children's programs, and shelters in the city. The program was not a flop. It provided food for my family all summer. I appreciated everything they did for us. I also know that God initiated it. Thank you Lord.

My children attended Public School #21 on Tenth Ave. It was the best grammar school in Paterson at the time. Their grades were excellent but began to go downhill when I was in school. Two of my boys began fighting with each other over little things. I tried to keep them separated by sending them into different rooms. Arguments were over things such as, he touched my shoe, or his hand was on my bed. Talking to them was like addressing a brick wall. One was the agitator, the other did not like playing those games. The agitator saw how easy it was to get his brother stirred up so he continued to do so. Since they would not listen to me I began punishing them. Children in their day played outside. My boys loved to be out of the house. Keeping them inside was their punishment. The fighting got worse. I talked about being brothers and standing up for each other to no avail. Replacing television with reading a book was a headliner. Reading was a quiet time; one could not read and fight at the same time. It didn't last long. Fighting became a bigger problem. Even sitting at the dinner table I had to intervene. I could not figure out what was going on between them.

I got them together and asked who started this fighting and why. Both said the other brother did. I watched and listened and knew who the culprit was. I said to one, you can not do what he does. Whenever he bothers you, I will handle it. It turned sour when I was standing there scolding them once again and they began fighting as I was talking, totally ignoring me. Okay, I took the belt to them both and sent them to bed early. I was tired of listening to it; tired of trying to reason with them, shouting, and being ignored. I brought them together to apologize to each other and start anew. Neither one would. They stood there looking at each other. It came to a point where I was hitting them constantly. I tried threatening them with getting hit with an ironing cord like my sisters and I did when we were young. I hung it up where they could see it thinking that would deter the fighting but it didn't. I became frustrated and told them I would tie a knot in the cord every time they fought. There were four knots in it when I finally hit them four wacks each. Nothing stopped the nonsense.

On the day I hit them their father was there. He sat on the couch ignoring their bickering until I jumped up and hit them. He did not like it. You have a lot of nerve, I said. How do you say you come to see your kids but do not pay attention to them? I do not need you to visit me. Their problem is their father is not interested in their lives enough to come take them to the park and throw the ball around, or go to the ice cream parlor. You could just sit and talk for an hour; yet you want to chastise me. He got up and walked out the door. I yelled as I followed him, yeah get out you good for nothing! He quit his job and started selling drugs to avoid paying child support. Why am I so bothered? I began to act as if no problem existed. I confiscated the door keys and told them to go outside when they wanted to fight and act like dogs. I instructed my daughters to lock them outside when they fought until I got home from work. This is one of the reasons I had to drop out of college which broke my heart. I loved going but would have to put it aside for now. Back at square one.

Recalling the fire we had in 1975 brought tears to my eyes. The attic was a place my kids used to get away from everybody. They would play their instruments up there and sometimes lay a blanket on the floor while reading. There was an old rickety lamp someone found in a closet that they used. My children are all avid readers. I would set aside time for reading for everyone at the same time. They chose their spot where they would not be disturbed. I asked each one when they were finished what the book was about. One day the lamp was left on and the wire got hot and smoldered through the floor. No one smelled smoke before we left in the morning. The call came in at work. My house was on fire. I am glad no one was hurt. My aunt said I didn't seem too upset on the phone when she called my job. Everyone at work thought I was joking because I was too calm. I explained I could not get too excited. I had to walk to the bus stop that would take me downtown to catch another bus. There was no straight line to my house. It would take time to get there and I had to keep my composure until then. One of my co-workers offered to drive me home.

Fire hoses were everywhere. I crossed the street to stand with the onlookers. The shock I experienced was not from the fire but from the way everything was structured. I had a dream the night before that the attic caught on fire. It may have taken the edge off of the situation and why I was not in a panic. I did not remember the dream until I was facing the house. As I looked up it was the same scene I saw in my sleep. I was standing in the same place looking upward. The firemen with hoses standing on ladders leaning against the house gave me a feeling of deja vu. Thank you, God, for the vision. It kept me from losing my mind.

We heard the school bell ring. Drawn by the smell and smoke in the sky everyone came running around the corner to see whose house was in danger. With tears in their eyes, my children kept asking, where are we going to live? The first floor only had water damage in the back room and kitchen. The attic floor caved in and fell to the second floor. A Fireman escorted me in to examine the damage. My living room was destroyed. We had a fifty-gallon fish tank that busted and fish were jumping everywhere. I was out of the house with six children. The Red Cross was there trying to console me. They wanted to put me and my children in a hotel but everyone kept saying no to that. The hotels they use are full of the homeless and people on drugs. I declined. After the firemen were gone, the people left, and we had nowhere to go.

My parents lived in the front rooms of their house because there was no water damage there. Having us stay with them overnight might have been disastrous because their ceiling could still cave in. I asked a family member if my boys could stay until I found out what I should do. Then I asked another family member if the girls and I could stay with them. There were four people in both families already. Both were reluctant. They didn't want to do it but agreed for a short time. I said put my boys on the floor if they fight. The girls and I slept on a closet floor. I thanked them for taking us in. I split my paycheck in half and paid them every week we were there.

My children went to our house after school. They sat on the porch to do homework until I came. I went to work because I had to pay for our keep. I could not just sit around. I spoke to my mother. She said to wait three days before doing anything. Someone from the Fire Department was coming back after a few days to assess the damage. Then they could have a contractor come in and give them an estimate of how long it would take to get the work done. I relayed that message and tried to keep the kids outside until bedtime, to not be a burden. How my family treated us was heartbreaking. They did not have any sympathy as to what we were going through. I would have taken them all in and doubled the kids up in the beds to make room for everyone. No one would have to sleep on the floor unless they wanted to. The couch is just as good as a bed and they certainly would not have to pay to stay with me. With the looks and cold shoulders I got I did not want to stay any longer than I had to. I was told my boys were not wanted there any longer. She had enough of her kids and my boys had to go. There was nothing I could do at the time. Children do not understand what you're going through, they think about themselves. I stayed outside with the boys until dinnertime then went back outside until bedtime. I gave them their baths and left when they were down for the night until I received some news.

The fireman said there was not much water damage and the walls would be fine. The contractor said we had to wait at least six months for everything to dry out completely. We could not stay where we were for that length of time. I called my ex to see if he had room for us. He renovated and lived in the attic of his mother's house. There was a living room, two bedrooms, and a bathroom. He wanted proof there was a fire before he gave me an answer. Why would I lie about something like that? Me and the kids were out on the street. Why would I want to live in his attic apartment when I have a whole second floor and use of the attic? I told him it would only be until they finished the work. He and some friends moved the furniture out so the work could be done and moved in with his girlfriend, which kept him off my back. I did not want any baby mama drama. We moved back home in less than a year.

All the furniture was returned except my sectional couch. He cleaned it and gave it to his mother who kept asking him for it because it looks new. How dare you give my couch away. Now we do not have anything to sit on. Is she more important than your kids? I was glad I had a job at that time.

Before I started working I had gone through a program at the unemployment office where they help you find work. When it was over I still had to go there every day. We would look through newspapers to see if anything stood out that we would want to do. The agents would suggest a job if they saw something. If we found something ourselves, we would show the agent. They had to decide if it was a good fit, we were not allowed to make that decision on our own. I will never get a job this way. I needed something immediately. I found a listing. The agent said that type of job is for teenagers and they are usually part-time. At this point, I was praying through trying to keep my hopes up. A new Welfare Caseworker was assigned to me. She was as ghetto as the day was long. Her call to me turned out to be an all-out argument. How do you call someone to introduce yourself as their new caseworker and wind up arguing? We set up an appointment.

When I saw her she was looking down on me with a smirk. She was very tall. If looks could kill I would be six feet under. Hump! Was her first reaction as she looked me up and down. Did you bring everything I told you to bring? She growled. I answered, I already knew what to bring. She was a black woman with a foul mouth and ratchet attitude. Every other word that came out of her mouth was a cuss word. As she snatches the paperwork and turns to sit I said, do not snatch anything out of my hand again. Why aren't you working? She asked. I explained the school situation, why I had to quit, and what I was doing at the present which was sending out applications. She told me to take whatever job calls first and let her know when I get one. I said I would call you just like I would anyone in your position, but I will take whatever suits me not you. We were not using nice tones with each other. She gave it to me. I gave it back. I signed the papers and left.

Applying for a job in Paterson was useless. Everyone turned me down. No one had openings. I was hoping for a position here so if anything happened to one of my children I would be close enough to get to them. I sent lots of applications out to surrounding cities. No one contacted me, so I went back to the item in the newspaper that I found hoping it would still be there. I informed the agent at the unemployment program that I was going to give them a call. She said I was on my own and she would cancel me out of the program. I needed to go to some interviews. I answered the ad and set up a meeting. I let my caseworker know what transpired. She wanted to know where and when. I was excited knowing I was going to crush this interview.

Here I am, I thought as I stepped through the door of an Eye Doctor's Office in Totowa, New Jersey. The two teenage girls behind the front desk were very friendly and polite. I was seated in a group of young ladies also competing for the same position. The Doctor came out of his office and walked to the front desk. He answered the phone and then walked back into the office. It seemed like every five minutes the same thing occurred. Whenever he walked back he would cut his eye toward the group. I was the oldest one there. I asked the girls whom they thought he was looking at. They all said in unison that they didn't know. The next time it happened he stopped and looked right in my eyes. When he went in I went to the desk and asked if there was a problem. I was told my caseworker keeps calling wanting to speak to the doctor. About what? I asked. She should not be calling here at all! The girl said she didn't know. I stood there with my jaw dropped looking at them.

The phone rang. Let me know if that is her on the line, please do not bother the doctor. I put the phone to my ear and heard in a very condescending voice, you better put the doctor on the phone now! I looked up at the young girl and apologized for the tone of voice and the downtrodden attitude of the woman on the other end. Who do you think you are? I asked. I tried to keep my voice muffled so it would not be heard throughout the office. First of all, you should not be calling here at all. She asked if I had been interviewed yet. I answered abruptly, I will let you know when that happens. You do not need to call the doctor. He has nothing to do with you, I hung the phone up. Once again the doctor came out of the office. I went up to him and apologized for my caseworker's conduct. His face was red. He was furious. The phone rang again. I took the call while he stood there listening. Yes, she called right back. I told her I was going to report her and I told the doctor to call the Wayne police to make a complaint against her. This was total harassment on her part and she should be ashamed of calling herself a grown woman. In the meantime, I heard her calling me all kinds of black bitches in my ear; no one could hear her but me. During my interview the doctor said, I was thinking of hiring you as a permanent worker in place of two part-timers. I will not go through this every day. I apologized! I assured him everything would be fine. I will no longer be in the program once I have a job. He said I looked over your records and am impressed with your education and the programs you've attended. He thought I would fit in. I was hired. I called my caseworker from the office. He did not want me to use the phone. I said the call should keep her from bothering you again after I leave. He agreed.

The office was on Rte 46 in a mall and the bus stopped right behind the building. Getting to work was no problem. The first day was a good one. The job was not hard and the doctor was a pleasure to work with. He was soft-spoken and compassionate, very easygoing. I took the job even though I would need another part-time along with this low-paying job. I needed money fast. It was a start. Two weeks later was the beginning of the following month. I received a check from the Welfare Department in the mail. What was this about, I thought? I had to take off from work to go down there to give this check back. My calls were not going through. The thought of cashing the check went through my mind. My sister said that is not a good idea. They will find out and you could go to jail for it. Yes, I thought of that too.

The next day I called in to say I would be late to work. Little did I know I would be sitting and waiting all day. At four-thirty everyone gets up and leaves. I asked one woman, where is everyone going? She said they are closed. See you tomorrow. The next day I had to speak to the doctor to fill him in on what was taking place. He remembered I told him there would be no interference from the Welfare Department. It is a mistake on their part. I am no longer in the program. I can not keep the money; it's not mine. With the check in hand, I enter the waiting room again and announce that I am here to see my ex-caseworker. The same people that greeted me yesterday greeted me today. I didn't feel so edgy this time because my boss knew where I was.

One woman started conversing about how something should be done about this caseworker. I told them what happened to me and how angry the doctor was. I do not know if I will have a job after today. On the third day, I tried to get information from the security guard in the hall, concerning speaking to someone in management over the caseworker. He said he didn't know who I could contact. I went back to my seat. The woman I usually spoke with asked what we were talking about. When I told her she said the receptionist, the guard, and the caseworker are all good friends. They go out to the club together, eat lunch together, and work together. They are not going to help you. I looked up in surprise. The guard and receptionist had their heads together whispering and laughing, while looking in my direction. I said I can't keep coming down here like this.

Back at work with things flooding my mind, I forgot about the check until I received another. I put it with the first one on the dresser. It was time for recertification and I received a notice. They sent a date to sign the paperwork and I took the checks with me. There were caseworkers at their desks but I did not see the main one I was there for. I asked the woman who was sitting right in front of me about receiving checks after getting a job. She said, Honey, you don't receive checks after you go to work. I said, I do. She asked who I was here to see. She looked toward the left of her which was around the bend from where I was standing. I could not see who she was addressing. The woman asks are you sending checks to someone who is supposed to be cut off? She comes around the bend, looks at me, and says she gets checks. I said well, I shouldn't. She said then why would you come down here to sign papers? That is why you called me but that is not why I'm here, I said. I come to give the checks back and find out why you're sending them when you know I am working. She said I didn't know you were working. Yes, you did! I said. You harassed the doctor until he hired me. The other caseworkers listened as we snapped at each other, giving their co-workers the evil eye. I said to the woman I just wanted to know who to give the checks to because I was not giving them to her. The woman said I had to go to court and bring them with me. Court! Why would I have to go to court when I have them and didn't open them? I held them up so everyone could see. She said that's the policy. We can't touch them. I said I can not keep them around the house and I certainly was not going to carry them around all day. She, along with one other person, said to deposit them and take the bank statement. I did that.

The process took so long that I forgot who gave me the money. I used to hold cash for people but could not remember where this amount came from. I was waiting for someone to say they gave it to me to hold and forgot about it. My refrigerator, stove, and washing machine all broke down on the same day. I purchased them together as a set. I was frantic. My boss would not loan me money and take a payment every week, so we survived without them for a while. The weather was cold so we sat food that needed to be refrigerated on the porch. I washed clothes in the tub with a washboard. Then I decided to use the money in my bank account to purchase new appliances and put the money back in increments. My heart was pounding out of my chest when I received a letter with a court date for Welfare fraud five years later. In court, all of this unfolded. The fraud case was shut down but I had to write a check for the amount I had in the bank and paid the rest over time. I heard a while later the three friends got jail time, not just for my case, there were others.

Ultimately, a new Eye Doctor's office opened up on Main Street in Clifton and I was transferred. The doctor did not want me to leave. I loved working at the new place mostly because the commute was easier. The manager was a young girl who thought she was privileged because she played guitar and sang in a country band. Flipping her hand while she barked orders and turned her back was disrespectful. You can not get me to do anything, treating me like that. I guess she understood when I didn't move. She told me she would write me up. Okay, go ahead, I said. The corporate office gave me a call. The woman with preconceived notions thought I did the wrong thing and accused me. She did not ask me what was happening but told me. The sound of her voice was condescending and exposed her haughty attitude. She must have thought she owned the business. I had to stop her from spewing her gibberish. I let her know I was not going to be treated that way. She said well, she is the manager. And that gives her the right to disrespect me? I asked. She has veered far from the point of management and you need to speak to her because there will be conflict. She will not be spitting orders, waving her hand at me as if she just commanded her slave. I asked how many times could we be written up before being fired. She said three times. I thought that would give me time to find something else.

The call did not stop anything. The young lady was getting beside herself with her haughtiness. She was the talk of the office. We finally had to hash it out. She was feisty. Her attitude was such that she would kick my butt. Bring it, sister! You have to bring some to kick some. The disagreement did not venture down that path but I was ready nonetheless. She left to go on tour and I became manager of that office. I had to fight for the raise that comes with the position. For some reason, I kept getting the runaround. I stayed in the position as manager for a few years and quit never receiving the pay raise that was due. Shortly afterward, I received a letter stating that the company was being audited and I had to fill out paperwork. A check for the raise they held back from me came in the mail right on time. God is good.

My step-grandmother passed away. She was predeceased by her husband for many years. She was the nicest woman you could meet and spoke in a soft voice. She loved to go to church with a strong belief in God as her savior. She and her only child lived in the two-family house she owned on Governor Street. Allowing us to call her grandma was a privilege. My mother and step-father decided they were not going to sell her house so they rented the apartments. He mourned his mother's death, taking it very hard. In a short time wanted to sell his mother's house and go to be by her side. He started drinking heavily and one year later died from complications of the liver and depression. I am sorry that his life ended the way it did. I can't help but feel somewhat responsible because they would not raise my rent, and my children were always a nuisance, infringing on their time. I heard them arguing about money on more than one occasion.

They came to me to ask if my daughter could move to their other house. She was a senior about to graduate and had a part-time job. She can if she wants to but only after she turns eighteen. His mother's furniture was still there so she would not have to buy anything. She was an "A" student all through school and was accepted into the Honor Society. She still carries a grudge from childhood. She ran away as a teen to get her way. I said I am not running after you. If you want to live here you have to obey the rules like everyone else. She thought she should have her privacy. You do not get your way or privacy in a house full of people. She could not understand I was her overseer until she was eighteen.

I smelled cigarette smoke and asked if she was smoking. She said yes. My family told her that it would ease her nerves. What kind of misinformation was that to give to a child? I said you did not ask me if what they said was true. You just believed them? She answered, yes. I was bewildered. I found out two of my sons were smoking also. I left them with this to ponder; God did not make lungs to be filled with smoke. It will affect your health later on in life. There will not be any smoking in this apartment or the attic, go outside. Now that my children are teens, everyone wants their bedrooms in the attic. I was glad when the Work Program passed in the high schools that allowed teenagers sixteen years and older to work part-time. I signed papers so the oldest could do that.

The others were too young at that time. I told them as long as they keep their grades up I would sign them up early. They were all "A" and" B" students eager to find a job. I would continue taking care of the house and they had to furnish school items, trips, dues, and clothes with the money they made. Having my children help with bills would be ideal but I would rather they saved up for when they get their own.

†

CHAPTER VIII

THE HOLY RIGHT HAND OF GOD

Repenting and fasting became a way of life for me. The Glory was on me and God used me. One day after work my sister, who lived around the corner, walked up to me as I got out of the car and said I was diagnosed with breast cancer today. Without hesitation, I put my hands on her chest and began to pray. I said, be healed in the name of Jesus! I told her she had to believe God had already done it and it would manifest. At that time, I was in the church highly anointed, laying hands on and praying for everyone. Whenever the relationship between me and the church was off again, Christ Yeshua remained my Savior. He uses me whether I am in church or not. I took prayer seriously and walked in my positions as prophet and intercessor. She came back with a report from the doctor that the cancer was gone. Indeed it was and it never came back.

The devastation of breast cancer struck our family twice. This time another sister came to me for prayer. With all the things she had done to me, I could have turned her away, but when Christ reigns in your heart, you do whatever He would do, which is heal. I laid my hands on her and prayed. I know it was God who led her to me in her devastation and I also thought it was a test for me. The testimony was the same as my other sister's. Her cancer had gone into remission but came back five years later and metastasized all over her body. He would not heal her again. We knew her time had come but her regression was slow. She suffered for a while.

I recall my sister's health was so bad that she and her four children moved in with my mother. To see her deteriorating was heart-wrenching. Her youngest son and my youngest daughter were the same age and both were graduating from the eighth grade. I am glad she got to see him graduate because she was praying for that. She finally went into the hospital and we knew she would not return. I received a call from a nurse one night after visiting hours. She informed me my sister was on her way out and wanted to see me. She gave me ten minutes to get there. My sister said the Lord stood at the foot of her bed and said it was time to go. She asked him if she could talk to me first. He permitted it. I asked if she was sure it was the Lord. At that moment He said to me, He was there. What do you want with me if you know you are talking to Jesus? I asked. She said I'm scared. The family tells her to hold on and He is telling her it's time. Your life here is sickness, I said. Did He say He would heal you completely? She answered no, You are in the best hands with Him. Then the nurse interrupted. She whispered, "You have to go now." I kissed my sister goodbye and thanked the nurse for allowing our visit.

The next morning my family called each other and met at the hospital. The nurse called and they were all there when my sister took her last breath. No one called me. Of course, when they got back, with a smirk and the attitude of we got over on you; they told me she passed. I let them know the nurse called and I went up the night before to say goodbye. That was a shock to them. Their jaws dropped. Who would think to do such a rotten thing as to keep me from seeing my sister before she died? My family, that's who. They did not mind asking me for prayer to receive something from God, yet talked about me all the time behind my back. There were times when one of my sisters and her husband would get into fights. She would call my mother's house and we would get in our cars and go break it up. We would tell him to take a walk or something. I remember standing by the stove cooking dinner when my daughter came in and said they were fighting again. I said I refused to do that anymore. I do not want you or your sister in anyone's car. I am not going and you are not going either.

My mother came up the backstairs and opened my door. She swung it so hard it hit the cabinet behind it and came back at her. She quickly put her hand up to catch it in time. I stood there stirring the pot watching the anger build in her. She put her hands on her hips and said, you're not going? No, I'm not, I said. She asked why. That question got under my skin. I put the spoon down. First of all my phone did not ring. She did not call me. I am not her mother. If the situation was on the other foot she would not come to my defense. I have a house full of kids and will be going through stuff with them. I do not need her drama. Without saying another word she turned and left. I thought she had a lot of nerve coming upstairs questioning me. I said I was not going, that should be sufficient.

At one point in my life, I was working three jobs. I had to take care of everything myself and try to put money aside. When my parents purchased a mom-and-pop grocery store around the corner from the house on E.19th Street. It brought more drama into my life. They both had full-time jobs so they paid one of my sisters to manage the place full time. They wanted us to be part of their vision. They were upset with me because I declined and it became an issue. It would've been a good idea to take the offer because it was close to home. I knew they were not paying what I needed. No one is responsible for taking care of my family but me. I had to work full-time, part-time evenings, and Saturdays to make ends meet. Over the years I found positions at a flashlight manufacturing company in Paterson, keypunching payroll. My next job was paying the bills at a Company in Passaic, NJ; and then a makeup Manufacturing Co. in Mahwah, NJ; each job paid a little more than the last.

It was rough for my mother to take care of her grandchildren after my sister passed. The kids hung out in the store after school and did their homework. When my mother retired she worked long hours in the store with my sister all day. I told her I would see to it that the kids changed their clothes and did homework before going out to play after school. She looked me up and down like she smelled a skunk and refused the offer. One day my mother and sisters held a family meeting at the store. No one notified me. I heard them come in after the store closed. It was late and the children had to get to bed. One of my sisters called me downstairs. I was surprised to see all three of them there. One sister spoke; we had a family meeting. I said, oh really! I am impressed we never had those. Then I asked, how could it be a family meeting when the whole family was not there? She told me they used a cousin in my place. You're right around the corner and you chose someone to stand in for me?

First of all, she could never take my place and most certainly could not answer for me. It was decided that I was the one to take my deceased sister's children off my mother's hands. What? I laughed and said, you decided! That right there is what's wrong with this family. If you had done it correctly each one of us could have taken one child. Immediately, she called out the name of the child she would take, and the others followed suit. I said, and you do not listen either. How dare you think you can make a decision for me and enforce it. I am not taking anyone so one of you will have to take two. She says she works long hours at the store every day. How would she get them to school? I responded, they will be in school all day. Bring them when you come and take them when you leave. After school, they can do what they do already. Another sister said, well I live too far. I asked, do they have schools where you live? Enroll them. The last sister said I told you Glo was not going for all this. My last words were, I have six children of my own and there are two of you who have none. Each of you could take two? I shut the door and went upstairs. They truly messed up my day.

Living in the neighborhood was good for the children. They loved it. It was hard for me. If I had enough money I would not have stayed in that house as long as I did. With every job, my mother would constantly get me called into the office or fired. She would call my job every day even after she was told by the manager I could not have personal phone calls. My children were always in her apartment and she did not want them there. She called me to handle it. I always told them to say hello, maybe have a little conversation then go outside or go back upstairs. No one wants kids sitting around their house all the time. When I am home, If I hear them, I would go down and tell them to go outside. I constantly told them their grandparents couldn't sit and visit with their friends. You live upstairs not downstairs! The food she cooks is not for you, it's for them and their company. They claimed they were not eating her food but that's not what she said. She would not tell them to go outside. She would rather call my job to have me do it. I assume she didn't want to be looked at as the villain. I would ask her to put one of them on the phone. I'm not doing that! she said. I told her I had already given them instructions. Tell them to do what I told them to do. This was our daily conversation. I got on my disobedient children about the same thing every day. Every time I told them not to do something they did it anyway.

My parents bought an above-ground pool. They said it was for all the grandchildren but I did not believe it. I thought they bought it to keep my children out of their house. It was a bad idea because they could not tell me who would be the watchman while the kids were in it. I became the joy breaker again and rightfully so. Everyone got in it when we had cookouts. One day I was in traffic but felt anxious about getting home. As soon as I entered the house I ran straight to the back of the house to look out of the window. Looking down at the yard, I only see my children in the pool, splashing around and screaming. One of my sons had his face in the water but his hands and feet were not moving. I yelled from the window, get him! I ran down the stairs and saw they were dragging him across the pool to the stairs. They had him under the arms but his head was still under water. I was frantically screaming at them to lift his head as I stood on the stairs to receive him. He began coughing, choking, and spitting. Thank you, God!

I pulled him off the stairs onto the ground. That's it! Everyone out of the pool! Shut it down! I explained to them what was happening. This is why adults have to be watching over children because you do not know what to look for or how to handle the situation. I told my parents again they could not get in the pool unless I was home. We've had problems with the neighbors giving cookouts for the church, who thought it funny to throw their paper plates and cups in the pool. Once someone threw broken glass in the pool that cut my daughter's foot when she stepped on it. There was no way to prove God's people did it because the kids in the neighborhood were jealous also and we were finding things in the pool.

As teenagers, one would think my children would have matured in their thought processes. They would still go downstairs. I wondered if they did not believe my mother did not want them downstairs or if they just wanted to defy everything I told them. My mother should not have to tell my children to go find something to do. That is my job. They did not listen and I was tired of talking. My daughter found out a little of what I was trying to teach her when my sisters and mother were yelling at her. She came crying to me. I asked her why I should defend her when she did nothing I told her. If she had done what I instructed she would not have been twisted up in this. I handled it knowing I was going to be dogged out after I left. Young people, in every generation, have a problem with the way their parents raised them. We are blind to our actions until we go through the same thing our parents did with our children. How would we know what the right way to raise a child is if we are children ourselves? I would not have minded skipping over the teen years altogether.

I overheard my mother say to one of her friends that she could not stand one of my daughters. I commented saying, I notice you talk about her the way you do me. She said I never talk about you! Yes, you do it all the time. It was supposed to be indiscreet, turning her back and whispering to the other gossipers and backbiters. She was nice to everyone but me. I believe she disliked my children because she had no love for me. I figured that I was the one out of her five daughters who fell in her footsteps. She sees a lot of herself in me. Her life was not a pretty picture. Most trials we go through come down through the generations. Besides the sins we commit ourselves, we can look back at our *forefathers' lives, from the third to the fourth generations, and see who went through the same things. If you do not see the connection in your generation it will be in the next. We are a broken family with generations of women at the head. When no man is head of household everyone in the house is uncovered. Satan pulled Adam out of place in the Garden by taking his eyes off God and placing them on Eve. God meant it all for good but we, His creation, failed Him.

My mother's side of the family tree discloses the absentee fathers. They were either not in the home or left the family unit. Single women raised the children. That in itself is a curse. It goes against how God The Father fashioned it. My maternal great-grandmother was married twice. I don't know her story. Her two daughters were from the first marriage. One of her daughters never had children. Her other daughter, my grandmother, had children from different fathers. A few of them didn't carry their father's last names. That also went down through generations. My mother had five daughters. I found out, in my twenties, that one of my sisters had a different father than the rest of us but had our father's last name. I have children that have the same issue. Only one of my sons has their father's last name. The others have the last name I carry. It doesn't mean they are not his.

The day my mother came home from the hospital she and my father had a huge argument. I didn't understand what it all meant. I remember, as I got older, one of my mother's siblings and I had a talk. They said think, who does she look and act like? Right away the picture popped into my mind of the man I thought it was. Now I know the real reason my father left. In all the passing years I never paid attention to how our features didn't match. Then I heard from a different source there was a discrepancy about whether another sister had a different father also. She didn't look like my mother or father but looked like my maternal grandmother's sister, whom she was called after. That gossip was hearsay without proof as far as I was concerned. We were all my mother's children and that is all I needed to know.

My father went south when he left us and remarried. He had five more children. His first three girls he gave the same first, middle, and last names as my oldest sister, myself, and the sister after me. The only way I could accept that type of behavior was that I believe my father didn't think two of my sisters were his daughters. He married for the third time. He and his wife had two children. He wanted to bring them as teenagers to meet us. I was upset with that idea. He did not take care of my sisters and me, or communicate with us all our lives. He now wants us to meet the children he raised, took care of, and still live with. That made my blood boil. They were welcome to come to the house. I spoke to his children. He kept edging me on to speak to him when I was ignoring him. He said you can say anything you want to me. I was holding it back for so long that I had to let it out. I have nothing against you. I do not know you. What I do know is that you were not here when I needed you. I let him know how good our stepfather was to us. I didn't feel any better but at least he knew how hurt I was, and at some point, he was needed in my life.

We all have circumstances that are not pleasing to God and we must repent and walk away from them. The Lord opened my eyes by teaching me to repent the sins of my forefathers. Repenting removes sin from the bloodline. I noticed things my mother said about me that passed down to my offspring. I also see traits from their fathers in them. If we examine ourselves as God tells us in his word we would not talk about anyone else. Some people, even family members might condemn me for being so hard on my biological father. I am not trying to please people by telling this story. I am trying to get through this life into a better one. Finally meeting my father helped me with that by breaking the yoke. I hope that bit of information will help someone else be set free. If you want to focus on my past, go right ahead. Keep talking about it. It will get you nowhere. With God on my side, I moved on. A few weeks later, my father had a massive heart attack and took his last breath, cleaning out a lot on 12th Avenue and Carroll Street in Paterson.

My children's father was a mechanic so I asked him to take me to find a used car. The talk we had on the way was about how the police came to his job to arrest him for non-payment of child support. He didn't have the money in the arrears so he begged his boss over and over to pay it and he would pay him back. His boss wrote a check on the spot. I said your boss does not have to pay for your mistakes. If you had taken care of your children up front that would not have happened. He worked hard to pay his boss back then quit his job and began to sell drugs to keep the welfare off his back. I can not believe he told me that he worked to pay his boss back but would not take care of his children before or after this occurred. He is trying his best not to be held accountable but he still has to answer to the Lord. There is a higher power and He sees everything.

I found a 1976 Pontiac Grand Prix. It was white with a dark red interior. It was nighttime when I found it. The car was pretty dirty, but somehow I knew I liked it. There may have been a tiny dent outside but the inside was perfect. When I went the next day to get it, it looked like a different car. The dealership washed the outside and cleaned the interior. It looked like new money. I asked if it was the same vehicle. The salesman laughed and said, yes it is. Four of my children had licenses at the time and they thought I bought a family car. They were all waiting on the porch when I arrived home. Working a full and a part-time job I needed transportation to get to and from work. Shopping on Saturday and church on Sunday were also on my list for needing an automobile, which took priority.

Dividing time to accommodate four teenagers was not the reason I purchased a vehicle. As it turns out each one had a weekend, which included Friday evening, Saturday evening, and Sunday evening to get the car. They had to fill the car with gas. There was a complaint that they would not use all the gas they put in and I would be using it throughout the week. I said yes, I am the one furnishing the car. Save your money and get your own! No one will use it if they are not going to put gas in it! If something happened I would be the one to repair it. I began hating that car and wanted to get rid of it. It was not available when I needed it or someone was arguing over what belonged to me. I let a guy I was dating drive the car just to keep it out of their hands. He abused my ride but I didn't care. I dropped him and the car.

All that happened to me during my lifetime, shifted my mind into a state of just going through the motions. Assuring myself that there was a way out is what kept pushing me forward. I didn't have the resources to exit the path I traveled. I waited to see what was at the end of the road. Fornication was my sin. Finding a permanent man in my life is not a thought in my mind even today. In my past men stalked, harassed, and even abused me. I lost all respect for men and I use the term men loosely. Not one of them was mature enough to know their purpose in life. Most certainly they didn't know mine. Maybe they came to me because they saw the depressed spirit possessing my life, or maybe they could see the hurt in my eyes or hear the devastation in my voice. I attracted that kind of spirit because of the mental state I was in. I never considered myself beautiful, or what people call sexy. I am a short average black woman who owns nothing. I live hoping to get from one day to the next. A man did not stay long in my life after I left my children's father alone. If anything was said to me I did not like, or something was said to my children, he was gone. If he talked about putting his hands on me at that moment it was over whether he was joking or not. Take that nonsense elsewhere. I had enough drama. I was not looking for someone to control me.

God gave men braun to do the heavy work. He never told men to beat women down. A woman longs for a man to take care of her which is the task God gave him. She is a gift from God. Eve is Adam's partner, his help, not his possession. Generally speaking, men have the mindset that "head of household" means they are in control of everything. God's word says he and his wife are to come together as one, not only sexually but mentally and spiritually. Working things out in agreement with each other. The word tells women to be obedient to a God-fearing man, not just any man. If I were not supposed to use my brain He would not have given me one. I think for myself, I do not need a man to do that for me.

God wants to be involved in everything we do, but just like in the garden, we humans want to do what's best for us. We want to be like God but independent of him. We are rebellious creatures seeking all the glory for ourselves refusing to align with the divine plan. I do not want to be bothered with men or marriage, so I asked God to take away any sexual feelings or conduct from me. He did just that. He said, "If you want to rid yourself of wrongdoing, repent and resist it to be forgiven." I began to work on that immediately. When He sees us doing our part, resisting sin, with our whole heart He will step in. I can testify I am free; the things I used to do I do not do anymore. Honestly, I believe God would not have done that if I did not have children already because he commands us to be fruitful and multiply.

Receive this message. When God's word is implemented in our lives it works. Continuing to do the same things over and over will bring no change. Regardless of how many times we enter the church, or tithe, or how long we pray, we are not considered His until we begin to live His word. No one can get you into God's Kingdom but you. Be received through the pearly gates of heaven by asking for salvation and having a change of heart and mind. The Bible says the path to destruction is wide, and many are on it, but the path to God's Kingdom is narrow, and few make it [Bible. Mat 7.13]. Some people say men wrote the Bible, not God. He is faithful to His word and whatever it says will happen.

Do not let any misconceptions you have concerning the Bible hold you back, ask someone. There is not much time left on this earth. I refuse to go to Hades because family members or friends are going. If I have to be on the path by myself that's the way it will be. When I turned my whole life over to Him true praise and worship became my new norm. The Lord and I have conversations every day. I learned so much from Him, certainly more than I learned on my own [Bible. Mk 4.2]. I always thought there had to be more than I was being taught in church. I kept asking God what it was that I was not grasping onto. Life is about God not about church. Assembling ourselves in the house of God has its purpose but one does not have to be a member of a church to find God. He is everywhere which means He can save you wherever you are.

CHAPTER IX

GOD'S HEAVENLY POWER PREVAILS

My daughters wanted to stay in the church I started them off with. I never took my sons back because they were humiliated and thrown out for disrupting the church when they were young. I was pregnant with my last child and was not feeling well that Sunday. I decided to stay home and let my two daughters watch over their brothers. Each one watches one. I told them if the boys act up, bring them home and go back. I thought everything went well until the service was over. The pastor called them up to the pulpit and mocked them making fun of their clothes and shoes. The church laughed. Then he said tell your mother not to send you back here. I forgot the exact words but this is close enough.

If I had to do it over I would not force them to go to church but give them Bible study at home myself. I was furious. To use one of my mother's phrases, "You could see the steam coming from the top of my head". I had every intention to show up the next Sunday and give them a piece of my mind. My daughters asked me not to because they wanted to continue going there. I had to think about it for a while. They could have taken up a collection. I surely needed it. This particular church had city workers as part of the congregation who were all in competition trying to out-dress one another. They were known for wearing fur stoles, mink coats, rings on every finger, with all the bells and whistles on every toe. Each one could have offered a dollar. A church full of pride and haughtiness could have been blessed by God that day. Stay humble church.

I praise and worship more at home than at church. I understood who the Holy Spirit was years ago by suffering from back pain and was healed immediately when I asked for it. I was confused about how the Holy Spirit entered my body yet I knew He was there. We think more of these bodies than we ought to think. I told family members about the healing. They prayed for me and I fell to the floor. I felt the Spirit of God enter me as I lay on the floor that day. I got up and started walking all around the house. I laughed so hard because I was not doing that myself. I kept saying I am not doing this! I can't stop! The Holy Spirit kept walking me to show me He was there. I got the feeling they all had to be shown more than I did. That experience was weird but funny. At that time I was away from church. After repenting I asked the Lord which one He wanted me to attend. He said the one on the hill. I knew which one He was referring to. I had family who attended there. Although I didn't need permission, I was told I could Come. The doors of God's house should be open to all who grace the doorstep.

I was on a mission in my new church home where the parishioners were well known for their missionary work throughout the city. The pastor was a white man who spoke softly. He had no music playing, no gimmicks, just his voice. The ambiance reminded me of Billy Graham speaking from the podium. The place would be filled with people hanging onto every word as silence filled the air. The first day we sat on the far left. There were a couple of empty seats for my daughter and I. We spotted my family members and gave them a little wave. None of them waved, nodded, or motioned with their mouths. For some reason, they kept looking over at us throughout the service like we were aliens.

I loved the way this pastor was serious about his teaching, no hemming and hawing, no theatrics, just the spoken word. I stayed at that church for years. The Holy Spirit showed me things that were not of Him, who were Godly people, and who weren't. He told me what to pray and how to pray. The devil is in every church. Satan is not going to let a group of people get together to praise and worship God and not try to stop it any way he could. I came up against the devil regularly. I found out that family members were talking about me which was nothing new, but telling the church I was the devil. I was shocked and didn't know what could have brought this on. Whatever was said the church turned against me and tried to get me to leave.

One day, while preaching, the pastor announced that the Lord had just told him to stop preaching, go home, and pack because he was sending him to Africa. The church went wild crying out No! No! Don't go! Tearfully he put the mic down, gathered his family, and left. The deacons filled in. One of the members fell sick and his wife asked the church to pray for him. She did not know what was wrong with him but she didn't look too well herself. We all prayed. In a short time both of them, and their two children, were seriously ill. She came up to me one Sunday and asked if I would come to their house to pray. She knew I was a warrior. She said everyone had been going every week after church to pray for her family. I looked around at all who were listening. Really! And no one told me about this. Yes, I said. I will come.

The table was arranged beautifully for dinner. Some, without washing their hands, went straight to the food. I stood and watched with my arms crossed over my chest. She invited me to eat. I said I didn't come here for that! She said we would pray after everyone had eaten. No, we won't! I said with an attitude. Some people put down their plates, others kept doing what they came to do. She showed me around. Her family could not get out of bed. They lost weight because they were not eating. The shapes of their bodies were imprinted on their mattresses because they'd been lying in the same spot for so long. Their eyes were sunken and had black rings around them. Coming out of the bedroom I noticed a staircase in the living room. She said it led to the basement that the landlord is now using as a separate apartment, but didn't close off the door. She said the people he rented to were satan worshippers. She saw shadows come up and down those stairs and didn't know what to do. They were speaking and performing rituals right beneath their bedrooms. I asked all those who were not eating to surround the staircase and pray in tongues while I went downstairs. I stood at the door like I was standing toe to toe with Satan and spoke to him directly. I rebuked him then commanded him to leave and never come back. After prayer, we ate. The next Sunday she announced that the people had packed up and moved that night. The church had been availing nothing because they were without the Power-of-God. He can't fill us if we are already full.

The Lord told me the pastor He was sending to us was from the State of Maine and was reluctant to come. That is what was taking so long. I laughed and said, now what do we do? " He said, "he's coming." Finally, the welcome committee picked up the pastor and his family at the airport, took them to the house, and out to dinner. There were a couple of days before church so the committee showed them around town. On Sunday morning, the house was full, awaiting the new pastor. We stood and clapped as he graced the pulpit. He stood looking back and forth in silence. I wondered if he was trying to spot a white person in the congregation. He said we don't have people that look like you where I come from. That was not the truth. My family lived in Massachusetts and owned three or four homes. The congregation was quiet. Then some laughed, and others yelled, that's all right! That's all right! They accepted him. I don't know if he accepted them. He continued to look around as he introduced his family.

My first impression of them was the total opposite of him. They were very friendly. He kept his eye on me every time he looked in my direction which caused the church to look my way. Ah! I thought this was going to be a challenge. The pastor got wind of the stories concerning me. A group of saints, if you will, wanted him to speak to me to get me to leave the church. He came to the overflow room where I was getting ready to leave after an evening service and asked if he could talk to me. He shut the door behind him and began to let me know I was not wanted there. You need to take your praise and worship home and praise God from there. Don't come back! He said as he waved his hands in the air, swerving from side to side to mock my praise. I left without saying a word because I had one of my grandsons with me. I will handle this later. A group of women stood smirking when I walked past them. A family member was one of them. She asked me what he said. I was not going to say anything, then I did. She was disappointed at how he confronted me but not because I was leaving.

The next Sunday I entered the church alone. At the top of the stairs stood my family looking down at me. What are you doing here? She yelled. When I reached the top I said, the same thing you're doing here. I was reminded I was asked not to come back. Oh that, I said. The Lord sent me here in the first place and told me not to leave until He told me to do so. Therefore, you could inform the pastor and your group, or click, or whomever. I turned and went to find a seat. Everyone was shocked to see me. One Sunday I had one of my granddaughters with me. While the preacher preached there were a few people from the Prayer Warriors Ministry walking around, laying hands on people. The woman from our section reached out to touch my granddaughter. I said do not touch her. She leaned over to touch me instead. I gave her the evil side eye. I asked what she thought she was doing. She said praying for people. Well, I heard you saying come out of her to one woman. That is not prayer and it's nothing to play with. You know spirits are transferable?

She moved to the row behind me and the devil began to growl at her when she touched some man's shoulder. She jumped back and everyone in the church began to run. I told my granddaughter to move up front. The pastor called for the men to all come lay hands on and pray for this man who was possessed. I got on my knees in the chair and the guy leaned toward me and growled. I put my hand on his stomach and he screamed. The pastor ran over, pushed me on the shoulder, and told me to move. No! I answered. He slid into the aisle with his back to me while the men prayed, laying hands on the man. Then I heard the pastor say he's free! He's free! No, he isn't, I said. The pastor was asked by one of the men how he knew the man was free. He said I just know! Then said get him downstairs. The men rushed him down. I told them how many spirits were possessing that body and how many were left. They all went into the room downstairs and locked the door.

The women call themselves chastising me. Let the men do it, one of them said. I told them to be quiet. It does not matter if you are male or female you have to have the power of the Holy Spirit. All of a sudden, it sounded like there was a physical fight downstairs, and someone ran out the front door screaming. The group of men came upstairs and said he ran away. That's not good, I said. They came to me and asked how I knew about the number of spirits there were possessing this man. I said the Holy Spirit told me. When you cast out spirits each one will go get seven more ferocious than themselves and return. So even though you cast them all out they will be back. Then what are we supposed to do? One man asked. After casting out spirits you pray a covering prayer over the person so they can not reenter. Spirits will also come after the ones who cast them out. You also must pray for protection over yourself. They asked me to pray for them right there. I did.

After the prayer, the men left. The pastor came up the aisle, pushed me from behind, and ran out of the church. I fell over the arm of the pew face down. When I pushed myself up the same group of women who consistently came against me surrounded me, including family. I said who do you think you are? You can not be women of God because you do not have discernment. You can't discern what is of God and what is of the devil. What preacher deliberately pushes a woman down and then runs out the door? They stood looking at me not speaking a word. I said get out of my way and you better not touch me. I left. As I walked away I prayed for God's people.

During the summer months, we go on a mission to every park and housing project in our city to pray for people. As the van was riding down the street we saw the young man who was prayed for at the church months ago and never came back. He looked disheveled. His eyes were sunken in, and he was riding a bike erratically, really fast on the yellow line in the middle of the street. The men wanted to continue their prayer but he turned down a different street. I said we can only pray God will send him back or He will do something in his life.

This particular week we were going to the Alexander Hamilton Public Housing Project on Alabama Ave, known as the Alabama Projects. A street gang had taken over the premises. They had the entrances blocked and were not letting people in or out except to buy drugs. Our plan was to stay on the sidewalk surrounding the project and pray. When we arrived, the entrance was not blocked, so we drove into the area. We saw people at the other entrance across the lot. We exited the van and formed a circle. Cars started driving through. They drove in, handed the person money, got their drugs, and drove past us to get out. As we grouped in a circle I said we are not here to stop or focus on what's happening. A couple of the women pointed their fingers for me to turn around. I turned and a young black man with a gun in his hand stood right behind me. He asked how we got in. No one spoke, not even the head of the ministry. There was no one at the entrance so we drove up, I said as I shielded the sun from my eyes. He asked what we were doing. I said some people who live here called the church to pray for them because they could not get out to get their medicine, go to the doctor, or go food shopping. We are here to pray and ask God to make a way for all who are inhibited. It will only take a few minutes and we will be out of your way. I turned my back on him and all the others had gotten back in the van. How is it possible I didn't hear them move? One can not be afraid to do God's work.

I put my hands on my hips and said you cowards! I waved my hand at them and said I will do it myself. In the scorching heat of the day, I began to pray with my hands raised, looking up to the heavens for all who were being held hostage in the confines of their apartment. The cars passing through stopped to hear what was being said. The others filed out of the van to rejoin me. The guy stood behind me with his weapon listening. I also prayed for him. When I was done I turned and said thank you for waiting, we're done. He watched us leave. The team could not get over my braveness. We are supposed to be children of God. He does not back down and neither should we. He protects us when we do things his way. You would be surprised at how many churchgoers passed through that day purchasing drugs, looking at me like I better not tell. God save the church!

Sundays at church there was always something going on. People were on point with their ministries. It wasn't the same ole hum drum weekly routine. We didn't know what the Holy Spirit had planned for us but we were there at His beck and call. He always showed up one way or another. A couple of my family members came into the church crying regularly, running to the pulpit and talking about what the devil had done to them all week. On this day, the church was full, and the pastor had just come to the pulpit as a family member stood at the back of the church crying profusely. She fell to the floor and proceeded to crawl toward the front of the church. Everyone waited. The pastor stood with his chin in his hand resting on the pulpit looking at me. I guess he was anticipating my intervention.

I raised my hands to God and asked, why? Why was it always my family? What is the devil doing to them that no one else experiences? I rebuke the devil in Jesus' name. I want it stopped now! I said. He answered, "Step out into the aisle and touch her belly." Then I stepped out. She saw me and screamed no! No! NO! Stay away from me! Do not touch me! Her arms were waving, and her feet were kicking like an infant getting their diaper changed. I bent down.

All the congregation made a grunting sound in unison. I touched her belly, stood, and went back to my seat. She immediately stopped crying. Thank you, Lord. One of the prayer warriors prayed for her at the altar. The pastor looked at me quietly for a few minutes then began the service. After church, my niece told me that when I walked down and bent over, her husband ran down the aisle, raised his hands as if to grab me from behind, and the Holy Spirit picked him up and threw him to the back; that was when the church made the sound. I was amazed and grateful, to say the least. Thank you Holy Spirit!

The first order of the day this Sunday was the First Lady's healing. She was diagnosed with breast cancer. The pastor called all the anointed women of the church to lay hands on his wife. Just about every woman got up and came forward. She was well-loved in that church. I went to step out and the Lord said, "Not you!" I stepped back. The pastor's eyes were on me the whole time. He was probably wondering why I stepped back. After the last woman took her seat I walked up to the front of the church. That was not an easy thing to do because the Lord had my eyes shut and an anointing on me so heavy I did not know if I was going in the right direction. He reached out my arm. I stood toward the back of her with my left hand on her left shoulder. The Holy Spirit drew a circle on her back with the tip of the forefinger on my right hand, as if He were cutting her open. He pulled down the flap, put his hand inside, pulled out the cancer, and threw it away. Finally, He made a gesture as if He was sewing her up. He turned me around to go back to my seat. It was totally quiet in the sanctuary. We went on with the service. The next Sunday, the First Lady announced she went to the doctor the next day, and he could not find a trace of cancer. Praise God from whom all blessings flow! He is the divine healer. It was a grand time in that church. The Lord revealed himself many times.

There were a few things that bothered me. Most of the time I was the only one who showed up on prayer night. If prayer is referenced as the most important time, why was that the night chosen to hold church meetings when no other time was available? On one occasion the congregation must have thought they could easily put me out. Only after I gave them a piece of my mind did I leave. They had to eventually give me a key because the person in charge did not want to come outside to open the church door anymore. She lived in the house next door owned by the church. I could not blame her. The Lord kept changing our prayer time. With every time change someone dropped out. Before long, it was just me, and I kept coming. I kept waking her up at all hours.

When we started this ministry, we would meet an hour before church, but that was not enough time to go home and do everything we needed to get ready and come back. At four in the morning, I put my coat over my pajamas with my hair in rollers and went to pray. Sometimes I almost got caught by staying too long. I would go home, take a shower, and come right back. Everyone felt the anointing when they walked in the front door and asked who prayed this morning. All were shocked when they were told I was alone. How could I be a product of Satan when he does not heal, pray to God, or confess that Jesus Christ is Lord? Hopefully, their eyes were beginning to open. Some were asking me to be part of their ministries. The Power-of-God is for His people but is missing in the church because of clicks, gossip, backbiting, jealousy, envy, and such. He is not about those things. He is about obedience, prayer, love and His church coming together as one.

Before long, the devil began to appear regularly, and the people had issues with the pastor. The congregation prayed about the situation and the Lord separated the church into three divisions and sent each group to a different church. There were maybe five people left standing with the pastor. One day, I stopped in to see if anyone was there because every time I passed by, it looked like it was shut down. I walked into a dark place, no lights were on. The sun was beaming through the stained glass windows. About eight chairs were in a circle with five people in attendance. The pastor turned and looked at me. I looked around for a few seconds and left. I prayed for him, his family, and his members.

✝

CHAPTER X

FAMILY REJECTION, GOD'S ACCEPTANCE

Cancer strikes our family for the third time. My mother was diagnosed with throat cancer the size of a quarter. She was a chain smoker. The ashtrays were always full when we were growing up. The doctor said he had to operate and was sure he could get it all and with treatment, she should be okay. Everything went just as the doctor said it would. The main instruction when released from the hospital was she could not smoke or drink again or it would kill her. I talked to her and reminded her that everyone comes to her house to hang out, drink, and smoke. I told her I would tell them what the doctor said if she wanted me to. She agreed. I suggested I go get a no smoking sign from the dollar store because the people wouldn't listen to me. She agreed again. I sat the sign on top of her floor-model television where all would be able to see it. I heard the noise when the crowd began to file in. I did not go downstairs right away so they could visit. I was beckoned to come sooner than I intended to go.

You would think when someone was just released from the hospital one would visit to offer any help needed and not stay long in respect to the person's need for rest. Not this group! They came with liquor and cigarettes in tow. I entered the living room saying hello to everyone. No one spoke and I did not expect a response.

As they lit their cigarettes my mother said take your sign down. They vigorously puffed on cigarettes to smoke up the room with smirks on their faces. I looked back and forth at them and then said, that's not my sign. You said purchase it. If you do not want it, move it yourself. Your life is at stake here not mine. Before I turned to leave I said you're killing her. You know she is not supposed to be smoking or drinking so why would you do those things in front of her? You ought to be ashamed of yourselves. I turned to leave while they poured drinks. Alcoholics are what I called my family, and friends whose daily ritual was to gather at my mother's house to drink.

I was on my way to the basement to do laundry one bright Sunday morning and stopped in on the first floor to say hello. The doorbell rang and my mother went to answer it. I heard the voice. It took a while to get through the hallway, but I could smell the liquor before I saw who it was. I peeked out in the hall and noticed the person was bent over at the waist with both hands holding onto the walls. Their feet were turned outward to the side and were walking on their ankles. That is a demon! I shouted as I pointed at their feet. I've never seen anything like that before. I told that demon to go, in the name of Jesus. My mother was stunned and never spoke a word. My advice was go to church and lay down on the floor in front of the altar. Call on Jesus to deliver you. I would hope a pastor would not let anyone walk into their church like that and allow them to walk out in the same condition, but it happened. The service that day should have started with a deliverance prayer over the members. The sanctuary is where God's work is to take place and prevail.

Another reason I did not associate with family was that my mother slapped me across the face every chance she got. I was never told why. Whenever it happened I turned from her and went to my apartment where I belonged. Do not think I didn't have visions of pounding her head against the wall until the blood poured out. I got angry at God because He allowed her to do that over and over for so many years. I would not speak to Him for a while but still prayed for her and the entire family. I rebuked the devil and prayed salvation for all. I had a strong feeling He was testing me each time. He and I always disagreed when it came to turning the other cheek. I could see Christians scoffing, and gnashing their teeth right now. I know you all do not want to hear that Yeshua takes us through situations and every facet of training to purify us. The devil has been defeated and has to ask if he can attack God's people. We give him too much credit for calling his name when things go wrong. God works out our salvation, not the enemy.

My mother moved into a senior citizens housing complex on West Broadway. It was a nice one-bedroom apartment and the people were friendly. We used the community room to have a family photo shoot since the cancer worsened. Not everyone showed up. We can never get the whole family together at one time. One of my nieces left a message on my work phone saying they found your mother slumped over the couch. She left no other information. I called the emergency rooms of nearby hospitals to find out where the medics took her. The whole family was in the waiting room when I arrived. I asked, am I the only one who didn't know about this? No one answered. I turned to go to my mother's room and someone said only two at a time can go in. I kept walking. My two sisters, a niece, and a nephew were there. I asked if she was awake? What happened? I was told she felt dizzy and fell over the back of the couch. She could not get up. It is not known how long she was in that position. It cut off her oxygen flow. The super of the building finally came to check on her as he did daily and found her.

My mother was complaining about her neck but wanted to talk to me. I had to bend over close. I could hardly hear her speak. She was trying to say something but I could not comprehend what she was saying. I beckoned my niece but she could not understand either. As I sat down on the bench the Lord spoke to me. "I want you to forgive your mother for all the wrong she has done to you." I thought to myself she must have been trying to apologize. I did forgive her but I did not care. I asked Him if her situation was serious. He said He was waiting for me to get there. My niece asked, what is the Lord saying to you? I know He is talking to you by the look on your face. I answered, She will not recover, it's her time to go. One of my daughters entered the room.

The day was dark and dreary. It was raining very hard. We were having a very bad storm. The nurse came to do a check-up and said it won't be long. We made sure everyone had a chance to say their goodbyes. When the time did come the Lord said, "Go to the window." I went and everyone in the room followed. It was raining so hard the window was gray, we could not see out of it. In a split second, the rain stopped and the sun shone bright like it was one hundred degrees outside. My niece asked what was happening. I said He is coming for her now. I watched Him walk across the sky as He kept His eyes on me. They all ran over to the bed, said goodbye, and kissed her. I watched the Lord walk through the wall over to her bed, and pick up her spirit. I said to the others, He is picking her up now and carrying her back through the wall. They ran back to the window. As soon as they passed through it became dark and dreary and the rain started to pour down once again. We stood there in amazement. The nurse came running in. He just came for your mother, she said excitedly. I have to check her vitals. She was gone. Cancer took the life of my mother.

My children were all over twenty-one. The oldest moved out when she turned eighteen and the oldest son took the apartment downstairs after my mother moved out. My youngest moved in with some friends and came back because it didn't work out. Everyone was doing their own thing. They come and go at will, and talk back as if they were more grown than me. It felt like I had several mothers and fathers but no one was helping to pay bills. I was too through with them all after asking, one night, if each one would chip in to buy food. They said no and turned and walked away. I asked the Lord when they would be moving out; He prompted me to speak to them at that time. I called my children to the living room to explain that I decided to get rid of the house. I gave them time to figure out if they wanted to purchase a house or get an apartment, and in the meantime save money. They were not pleased at all. The comments were flying especially from one who thought she could tell me what to do and have me do it. I told her she should have moved out already. I was sick of the attitudes. I was not putting them out in the street. I told them to prepare. Everyone older than eighteen should have been preparing already. My lifelong dream was to move out of that house but never had the resources to do it. I could have found a place of my own and left the responsibility of the house to them. My thought was if they would not put in a couple of dollars apiece to get dinner how could they handle running a house together?

The Lord took me out of work on May 4, 1998. I did not wake up planning or knowing I would leave the workforce that day. It was bright and sunny and the anointing was high that morning. I was praying and singing "It's all over me." I was in a good mood. There was a red cloud that followed me from Paterson to Mahwah where I worked in the office at a makeup warehouse. At my desk, before I started my day, I looked out the window and could not find the red cloud in the sky anywhere. I chuckled thinking maybe it followed me to work and then disappeared once I was safely inside. All morning I talked to the Lord, mostly in my head, ignoring everyone around me. I expressed to Him that I was done with working for people and wanted to work for Him exclusively. His silhouette appeared outside the window where I sat. I looked up and He said, If that is true, shut down the computer and tell everyone you quit.

I sat there looking up at Him dumbfounded. I said in my mind, now? Are you kidding me? I have a house and a new car to pay for. Two weeks prior the Lord allowed me to purchase and drive a new car off the lot. He assured me He would take care of me. I knew He would. His word says He would and I believe in and stand on His promises. That afternoon about two pm I made the announcement. I signed out and left the premises. I never told my children what transpired. They knew I was out of work when they saw me home every day.

Three months passed, and my anxiety was high. I found out that it was not easy sitting at home. Waiting on the Lord was a challenge. I am not saying there was nothing to do. There was plenty of work around me that I was not getting paid to do. I was afraid of not getting the bills paid and the house going into foreclosure. Every time I pray, I am waiting on you Lord! There was no response. By August I was done. I could not wait any longer.

I decided to find a job then the Lord spoke to me. "I will take care of you. Do you not believe it?" Oh, I believe it, I said. You didn't give me instructions on what to do in the meantime. He told me to focus on my prayer life. He gave me names of people to pray for, times to pray, and different ways to pray. I became so engulfed in prayer that I forgot about any problem I had. The Lord was with me, teaching me. In the living room, I had two wing chairs, a table between them, and a lamp that sat on the table. I said, Jesus, you are here every day. You might as well sit down and put your feet up, as I pulled the coffee table over to rest his feet. He laughed and said okay, "What else do you want me to do?" I said pray with me. He asked me if I was sure I wanted Him to do that. I said, yes. He asked again and I answered yes again. He told me to turn around and get on the couch on my knees. I stood up, turned around facing the couch, and knelt on the pillow with my hands folded on the back of the couch and ankles crossed. He said begin the prayer. I began my usual opening of prayer with my head bowed. I felt Him lean over and cover me. The power of God engulfed my whole body. I could not continue my prayer because I could not move anything, not even my tongue. He began to pray.

His prayer was of an incredibly high-pitched screeching sound, He prayed so fast it sounded like He was rolling his tongue. Within that sound, I could understand every word. With my body in a state of fear. I felt useless as if my life was meaningless. I was afraid of it and wanted to stay in it at the same time. After the prayer His power moved from me; yet I was still positioned for some time. My body felt like a bowl of jelly once I was able to stand on my feet. It was the most humbling experience. My daily morning prayer began with laying prostrate for two hours from that moment on to give honor and glory to Him.

Whenever I cast down a spirit or laid hands on those who were sick, I would be attacked. I was able to smell the spirits beforehand. The closer they came the worse they smelled. The Lord instructed me to stay still the first time it happened. They moved all over me. It was an eerie feeling. One was on my head and moved slowly over my face down to my nose as if to smother me. There was nothing they could do to me because He protected me. As they left, the further away they got the smell became fainter.

†

CHAPTER XI

DOING IT FOR HIM

Ironically, the Lord sent me into churches where the heavenly power is supposed to manifest. I was resented by the saints. I was looked down on, called names, and belittled from the pulpit because I had the authority to use God's power and they could not. The power is for all God's people to tap into not just those in the pulpit. If you are jealous it will not come upon you. One has to be in a certain place with God. He told his disciples in the book of Mark Chapter Nine to fast and pray.

A conversation took place between myself and a couple of churchgoers. I told them about the Lord taking my spirit to heaven. That story somehow reached a friend of the pastor, who is also in the city of Paterson. That Sunday she came as a guest speaker with a word for the church. Praise was high that morning and the Lord gave me a prophetic word for the church before the guest speaker began to address the congregation. She gave the scripture where her word was coming from then proceeded to point her finger at me and call me a liar. She said she did not believe my spirit was taken to heaven because she had asked God for that but it had not taken place. She was positive that if it did not happen to her there was no possible way it could happen to me. I never responded to her insecurity. Persecution is real in the church. Our minds and hearts are filled with envy focused on persecuting people. How about we love each other instead? God's plan is designed so that we all walk in His power. Figure out what is stopping you from reaching that point. Condemning others for having something you do not have is not a Godly attitude. Ask the Lord what you need to do to receive it. He wants us all to be on one accord.

Look at God! Everything the pastor preached I had already spoken prophetically. It was confirmation to the people. In these last days, the church is overrun with sin that His power can not shine. The church has the wrong outlook and needs a new mindset, a new focus. Nothing is about us, it's all about Him. Those who are prideful, envious, jealous, haughty, gossipers, and backbiters will never get there. They want all the glory and the glory belongs to God alone. His word says, "We can't serve two Gods. We must choose one and hate the other" [Bible. Mat 6.24]. The church thinks it's alright to be with Satan sometimes and then be with God at other times. The Bible calls it adultery. It is unacceptable.

Living with the enemy is easy and joyous. He lets us do anything and everything we want as long as it is not what God wants. Repent and move away from him. Nothing is free! Whatever we want in the righteous Kingdom there is a prerequisite to receive it. Salvation is not free. Whoever claims to belong to God and does not keep His commandments, is not His. He will continue to love us, bless us, pray for us, and stand by us until the end. He does that in the hopes we will change our ways. He will put up with our disobedience until the end. At that time if we have not turned away from the sins we commit He will say, "Depart from me I never knew you!" [Bible. Mat 7.23]. Folk today say God knows my heart! He will not leave me behind. He also knows you promised you would change but have not done it yet; So you are speaking it with your mouth but it's not in your heart.

I remember when the Lord asked me how I felt about martyrdom. He informed me that it is my calling. I was once told by a Christian woman that we have to go through this life like Jesus did. She said He does not call for us to die physically, we only die spiritually because of our sinful life. She was wrong. I never understood why anyone had to die since He died for us and that was once and for all. He asked me, if I were going to be killed because I knew him, would I deny Him? No, I would not deny you, I answered. I just want to know what purpose does martyrdom serve? It could never match up to what you have already done. He answered, "The purpose would be to cover and ensure the salvation of those you stand in the gap for." Again I questioned, Why can't the ones I stand for receive salvation the way I did? I know you are God and you see to it, through your churches and intercessors, that everyone is prayed for. You cover those who do not pray and those who do not know you. But I thought we all had to do the same thing to receive salvation. He repeated once again, "You were chosen! It is your calling."

"Now, watch what you say because it will manifest before your eyes. I do not want you to curse anyone's life. Pray the goodness of God upon them. Speak life and not death into every situation. When you pray for healing you will have to take on whatever you pray for and I will remove it from you." That's a tall order, I said. I am not sure I could do it but all I can say is that I'll try.

The Bible says He tests our faith, trust, and belief in Him by taking us through situations that will bring out the truth. He also wants to see if we will choose Him in these situations. Yeshua said there were some things I had to go through on my own. At first, I did not know what was going on. I thought the devil came in and snatched me up again but I knew it was the Lord. He did not answer or do anything to help. I felt like I was alone. Some things I went through sent me backward and others held me at a standstill which taught me I could not do anything on my own. I learned to just stand through the trials, continuing to pray and rebuke the devil. If the trial does not make an impact on us, we will go through it again until our eyes are opened to whatever He wants us to learn.

Everyone had moved out and I was in the house alone. I kept hearing a voice in my head say give it all up. I called on the Lord to ask what it was about. He said, "Would you give it all up for me?" I said without thinking, yes. "Then do it!" He said. Do what? I was puzzled. "Give up everything you have." Oh okay, let me see. What do I have? I have a new car I only drove for three weeks. I gave up my job. He interjects, "The house." But where will I live? "You trust me don't you?" Yes, and I can see the trouble you're going to get me into because of it. Then I laughed. He said, "Every bank account, every insurance policy, all the furniture." I was no longer laughing and my head was spinning. I did not know where to begin.

First I called the car dealership. The gentleman on the other end said, did I hear you correctly, you want to give the car back? Yes, Sir, I said. He connected me to someone on a higher level to handle this call. I told him I was no longer working and didn't know how long before I would find another job but did not want this bill going into default. He said he would have the car picked up. Two days later the repo man came to tow her away.

The instructions he received must have told him to just pick up the car. When I came out and handed him the keys he was stunned. I said it's not a repossession, I told them to come get it. The neighbors were asking why. What's happening? I ignored them. He stood and watched until I went into the house, never uttering a word. This was mine to do.

I redeemed my insurance policies next which was nothing but drama. The insurance agent was frantic. He was trying to figure out a way to manage the policies to keep them active. He did not want to pay. I said it was my money. He calmed down a bit. I did not know what he had to go through on his end but this had to be done. He suggested we do a couple at a time. I agreed as long as it gets done. I did not care what anyone thought. I was being obedient to my God. My faith, trust, and belief are in Him not in people. I wonder how many believers would go this far to show their love for Him. I heard of people who did this very thing.

I called the bank to settle the house. The gentleman I spoke to said he would get back to me. The Lord said, "Give things inside the house away to the neighbors." I had a mixture of new and old items. I notified family members that they could take what they wanted before I gave anything away. Two nephews came; one took the dining room set and some dishes. The other took two winged living room chairs. All others ignored me because I was parting ways with the house. They thought I should keep it because it was once my mother's. I had the house for ten years. My mother put the store on the market, moved into a senior's apartment complex, and sold the house to me. The neighbors wanted to know how long I would be living there. They didn't want to take anything if I was still occupying the house. I was trying to get rid of everything so I could leave. A catch twenty-two it was. I became furious and aggravated over the whole packing situation. The Lord said, "Put it all out on the curb."

The attic, basement, and apartment were full of stuff we accumulated over thirty years. The Lord said, "Just do it. I am going to take you to a nice house." That is when I packed my things, marked them up, and set them aside first. As I waited for further instruction I brought boxes and started in the basement. There was so much stuff in the rooms down there. I swept the cobwebs and filled the boxes. Taking them up the stairs and out the back door to the curb was time-consuming. Dragging those boxes did a number on my back. Getting up the stairs was the main problem. I could not lift heavy items. Each time I reached the curb there were little pieces of cardboard strewn everywhere from the previous box. Everything in it was gone. It was a very hot day; I was achy and sweaty. No one was outside but me. I looked around and then yelled, you are welcome to come inside to see what I have! Come on in! I shouted as I waved my hands in the air. I went to get the broom to sweep up the mess outside and continued the next day. The attic was like a steam shower. I did not want to venture up there but that was not an option. I stood at the top of the stairs in awe. A huge cardboard box in the middle of the floor was filled with footwear of every size. Where did they get such a large box? The shoes, boots, and sneakers were piled high above the top of the box in the form of a pyramid. This was done on purpose. My children were angry and thought they would get me back. I can only do what I can do.

I threw those without a match on the floor. When I came upon the other shoe I put them both in the same box, drug them down the stairs, and out the door to the curb. I did not know if the footwear could fit anybody but somebody is about to have a house full of shoes right now. Neighbors did the same thing as yesterday. The boxes were torn into bits. Not a shoe was in sight. I had double work sweeping again. Why the people just couldn't come inside. With my hands on my hips, I looked around. It seemed as if I didn't make a dent in the amount of stuff that needed to go out. My back was hurting. My hair, nose, and clothes were full of dust and I was drained from the heat. I was done for today. The money I received from emptying my bank accounts and cashing in policies paid the bills off.

I heard the Lord's voice again, "When the time comes your oldest son will be there to move you." Each day I cried telling the Lord He was taking too long. I did not sleep well. I was the only one in the house and every creek awakened me. My next step was to call the mortgage company. They told me to call the bank. I pulled out the mortgage papers and found the information and the person to contact. After giving the gentleman the rundown of everything, he said, repeat it again. He asked if I knew how many years it's been. No one wants that property! He did not want to speak to me and told me not to call anymore. I had to do what the Lord told me to do so I called the bank every day. They put me on hold and passed me around from one department to another for months. I was trying to get something accomplished before my phone was turned off. Whenever I talked to the Lord, He said, "Just give it back! Just give it back!" Hearing those words made me frustrated and angry. I told no one what I was going through.

My daughter asked if she could move back in to save enough money to get her apartment. I said yes but it was uncertain if she would reach her goal. I informed her that we may have to move before then. In the evening when she and her son were moving in, the electricity was turned off. Her son's father helped bring in their belongings. She asked where we could plug his television so he could watch his kiddie shows. We laughed. I said anywhere I guess; forgetting the lights were off. They tried every socket. Nothing worked. She went downstairs to the first floor to see if the electricity was on. The apartment was empty. My son had it turned off when he moved into his house. I heard them whispering in the dining room area, which was dark. I was sitting on the couch watching the TBN Channel on my TV. She said none of the sockets work in the whole house except the one where your television is plugged in. I said plug it in there then but it did not work there either. It was not until she asked how I was watching TV when the electricity was turned off that I realized what had taken place. I laughed so hard I could not speak. I forgot I told the Lord the only way I would stay in this dark house alone is if I could watch the Christian Church Channel. I tried different channels and nothing else worked. They stood there looking at me while I laughed uncontrollably. It's the Lord, I said. He did what I asked Him to do.

One of my sons asked if he could come back for the same reason she did. I told him we may have to leave in a hurry but you could stay until then. They both had time to save money and leave. I could not leave. I was still waiting on the Lord. Finally the bank returned my call. I spoke to the same man I gave my information to the very first time. He was rude. You are disrespectful, I said. Why are you so aggravated, I asked. He answered, What do you want, lady? Why do you keep calling us? I already told you. My situation has not changed. I am waiting for an answer as to what I can do. This is my life I am concerned about. I should be the one aggravated and pulling my hair out not you,

Okay he said, I will enter you into the Give It Back Program. My mind instantly focused on how many times I heard just give it back. What program is that? I asked. A program where someone is in dire need to have us take the house back. I said then why didn't you tell me instead of letting me go through that misery? He said you had to be asking for a certain length of time. They had to wait to see if my situation changed. I could have gone through the phone and given him a big kiss when he told me my name would be removed from the property, and I had to be off of the property by November 9, 1999. We are putting the house up for auction, he said. There will be people looking at it in the meantime. I was so relieved. A weight was lifted for sure. Albeit the house was now taken care of I had to deal with the furnishings that were still in it. No one responded to my invitation to take whatever they needed. No one called or came to see if I needed help. What do I do with all this stuff? I didn't know what to keep because I didn't know where I was going. Even that was a mystery.

It was the Friday before I had to be out and no one came to board up the house, or anything like that. I called the bank to find out what to do since no one came or contacted me. What are you still doing there? he screamed. Well, in this neighborhood when there is an empty house people will take pipes or anything of value. I was calling to tell you that and ask if you were boarding the house up. He said, oh! Thanks for making me aware of that but you must leave.

The next day my son arrived with a U-haul truck and some friends just as the Lord said he would. I was shocked because he never said he was coming. Do you know where you are going? He asked. Fighting back the tears I said, No. I can take you to my house until you know but you have to leave here now, Monday is the ninth. We can put your things in my basement but you can't take everything because it's small. I had to pick and choose which boxes to take. I made instantaneous decisions that left a lot of personal things behind.

What a relief, the house is no longer my responsibility. The new owner knew my son's ex-girlfriend. He told her he spent a lot of money on the removal of the stuff I left behind. That is what happens when you purchase something as is. At fifty-two years of age, I had no job and no place of my own to live. Who would want to move in with their children after finally setting them on their path in life? Not me! This is where God had me stationed. I tried with all my might not to scream at God and curse Him. That's the space my head was in. I'm keeping it real. I felt let down and discarded. I kept saying over and over in my head I am not doing this, I am done. Then I thought again I must be obedient.

My son has a nice one-family house in Paterson, NJ. Things were going well in the beginning, but I still felt displaced and unwanted. Living with someone when I had no income was a difficult place to maneuver. When you are down and out no one wants to see or hear you. You are mistreated and misunderstood. I was too young to receive social security and the Lord said do not apply for it. The anger in me was at staying level, No matter how hard I tried to release it, it stayed. Every time I thought about how the Lord tricked me, tears welled up in my eyes. I did not want to hear His voice, yet I wanted Him to say something, anything. The day He finally spoke I was told to cook and clean for my keep. What! No! I was dumbfounded. Now that I was free my new rule of thumb was to do those things when I wanted not because I had to. I was trying to put the old life behind me. When you have small children, cooking and cleaning are daily chores. He was keeping me in it.

My son had no time to do those things he worked hard and put in a ton of overtime. I could understand why I was stationed there. God does not do things one-sided. We both would benefit from it all. The times my son went food shopping he asked if I needed anything. I told him not to worry about me. He never went to the store for me when he lived with me and I was counting on this to be a short stay. He was single, worked every day, and did everything himself. What was I doing there? I stayed confined to my room, hardly uttering a word. After a while, I could sense tension in the air and felt it in my stomach. My sons and daughters got together and decided to buy me a used car. I guess to get me out of the house. I was deeply depressed and he had gotten to the point where he did not want me sitting around his house. I could not blame him because he was a depressed person himself. That is something he blames on me. The father is never held responsible for any wrongdoing. The mother catches it all. Children have a problem with their parents because the parents are the ones who tell them what to do and chastise them. My children are very negative concerning me. They did not want to do anything I said. Any instruction I gave was disregarded and they did what they wanted. It's called disobedience no matter how you look at it.

A couple of years passed and I told the Lord I was going to leave on my own. Of course, I had to get a job first but I was willing to do that. I reminded him of what He told me previously. You said you were taking me to a nice house but I did not know it was someone else's. You also said you had something for me to do and you haven't given me anything. "I gave you something to do. Cook the meals and clean so he does not have to do it." I responded to his statement because I truly wanted to understand. In a heightened voice, I said, so you took me out of work and out of my own house to put me in someone else's house to cook and clean for them! Okay, now I get it. I was being sarcastic. Before I moved the Lord asked me what were the three top things that I never wanted to do again. After thinking, I said cooking, cleaning, and living with other people. I gave that response because I had a lot of children and constantly did those things. I needed a break from that life and wanted to live by myself and cook and clean when I got ready, not because I had to. He put me in a position where I have no money, no place to live, and no assets. I am dependent on someone to put a roof over my head. This is His plan; I am being obedient to His command. No one understands that. As long as it was for a short stay my son did not mind. As time started passing he became irritable.

My stomach was in knots daily worrying about why I was still there. Heaven was not on my side. I lay prostrate praying every day for two hours or more early in the morning. My son left for work then I started my day. I would clean the house, take a shower, and leave until it was time to go to bed. I did not have money for gas so I would go as far as Garret Mountain and park there until it was time to go back. I would walk the path that goes around the entire park sometime and other times I was at the overlook area gazing out at the city. I started taking my Bible with me to sit in the car and read. His daughter loved being at her dad's house so she was company for me when she came. I watched her whenever he had somewhere to go. As the days went on, my depression sank deeper.

There were times when I sat in the bedroom with the door shut wanting to jump up screaming but had to hold it in so no one would hear. Other times I felt like throwing something against the wall but it was not my house. I was not in a position to pay for damages. I felt like running until I fell off the end of the earth. Who am I? What am I doing here? Whenever I felt like this, tears would automatically fall from my eyes without any effort and I could not shut it off. Having a car helped me get away for a little while but they do not run forever. I tried very hard not to overuse it to keep it running longer. Gas and repairs were paid for by my son which I thought was unfair. He does not drive the car, that's what I told the Lord. I wanted a job to pay for the expenses of the car. He only answers me back at times when I'm fed up and threaten to look for a job. He speaks only to remind me not to look for a job or leave. "I am the one who is in control," He says.

My sister developed diabetes and had to take dialysis treatments at the hospital. She was a cancer survivor. She and her daughter lived together with her daughter's two children, and a granddaughter in her custody. My family and I used to attend Madison Avenue Christian Reformed Church back in the day and this sister stayed with them. She loved her pastor and the church. All of our children went to Bible Study there every summer. On the days when she was too sick to go, I went to their apartment where we would pray. Sometimes, the Holy Spirit would enter, and we would have church. They wanted me to come over to do this more often. I agreed. There was praising, worshiping, and laying on hands. We had a grand time.

My niece was on the phone with her prayer partner one evening and asked if I would speak to her. Immediately I felt an anointing through the phone. She was telling me and I was telling her the same thing at the same time. We laughed. She asked me to pray for her church. They had just come off of a fast believing for some things. I told her let me pray and I will get back to her the next day. I had a whole regiment I went through for important things, and I prayed early in the morning. She agreed. I promised my niece that I would visit the church before the phone conversation took place. As God would have it, some of the church members showed up at my sister's house after work the next day to hear the word of the Lord. We were introduced to each other. They began to sing and the Lord took over. I prophesied for the church as a whole and some individually. He answered their prayers. We met like that at the house for a few nights and praised Him, then I went to visit the church. I was introduced to the Bishop, who was my height and spoke with a soft voice. She was a very gentle woman. She invited me to come back any time. It was my pleasure.

Once my sister's treatment began, it seemed like she got sicker, and her body started deteriorating. I was there to take her to doctors and dialysis appointments. I stayed with her which allowed her daughter to stay with the children. They moved into a larger apartment with an extra bedroom. The kids were playing one day and somehow shattered the glass of the breakfront in the living room. The announcement was made for everyone to keep shoes on their feet. No one realized my sister stepped on a piece of glass. She felt pain in her ankle. With diabetes, she had no feeling in her foot. The doctor sent her to the hospital to have tests done and found a sliver of glass that had moved up from her heel close to her ankle. He decided to move the glass down with whirlpool treatments instead of operating on her. I took her back and forth and waited through the treatments daily. We spent a lot of hours in the hospital until the sliver of glass came down far enough to use a tweezer to pull it out. As her diabetes got worse she was in and out of the hospital. Her daughter would take the children to school, then go to the hospital and stay until I came about two o'clock in the afternoon to relieve her. She had to tend to her family. I would stay most of the time until visiting hours were over. We kept that routine every time she was admitted.

Her condition worsened. It seemed like she was walking one minute and the next she had to have help doing it. She reached the point where she could not take the bus to church any longer. My niece had to stay home to take care of her mother. The process seemed backward to me as I watched the nurse administer treatment. I would ask questions, and she would explain. I want to say this, medicine does not heal anyone. It is a bandage that covers the root cause that no one deals with. If it did heal we would all be cured and live without sickness, illness, and disease. The doctors prescribe medicine to fix one problem but it comes with four side effects. Now five things have to be treated. That is why I do not take medicine. What I found out about diabetes and cancer I wish I had known back then. These were the times I wish I had studied natural remedies of ancient times.

I was awakened by the Lord one Sunday morning. He said, "Get up. I want you to go to church today. They start at eleven and you have to leave by ten." I quietly moved around so as not to wake anyone in the house. On my way out the door, I asked what direction am I going. It was cold out and I hoped it would not be far. I made a left at the corner from the house. Two blocks down the Lord asked, "Do you see that big tree on the next block?" "Keep your eyes on it." The tree was tall, full of leaves, and towered over the top of a house. As I got closer He said, "Watch this." All of a sudden, birds began to leave the tree, and it stood bare, not a leaf in sight. I was bewildered! Who knew that was birds? He guided me step by step the whole way without telling me where I was headed. I found myself across town in front of my niece's church and went inside. She did not tell me she was not going to be there that day. Afterward, I went to tell them what happened in church. My sister asked me to come by every Sunday because she wanted to hear about the works of God. Her daughter took such good care of her I thought she would make a great nurse.

I went to church every Sunday and brought back the good news. She was elated each time. I prayed for healing just as I did when she had cancer. This time was different. I cried out to God daily. Why isn't my prayer working? She loved the Lord and loved the church. I remember receiving a call that she was in the hospital. When I got to the hospital after work her room was filled with people. I again was the last to know. The Lord used another niece to give a prophetic word at her bedside. He said the same things He had me tell her several times in the past. He did not want her to participate in family gossip. "Stop taking the calls," he said. He also told her that He was the one who sent a prophet to help her. Then I said, which is me. I am that prophet! Everyone heard the message. She used to stick up for me in the family free-for-alls. I do not know what happened. Unfortunately, attitudes stayed the same.

The Lord kept telling me He was about to do something in my life. He speaks in one dimension, but in our world, it means something else; for instance, if He says now, it could mean five to ten years to us. If He says soon it could mean ten to fifteen years, but it will come to pass. In retrospect, whenever He mentioned the word, soon, to me, it took at least ten years. I wish I had known that information when I was going through it. He leads us into situations. Our mission is to push through and come out of it. If you keep going around in circles, doing the same thing over and over, you are stuck because you did not learn what He was teaching you. Step back, and ask yourself what is it I am supposed to do or not do? It's a test and we must pass the test. The Lord tests our faith and trust in him and our obedience to Him. We are humbled through it all. I failed many tests until I started looking at myself, what I had said or done, and taking credit or blame for my part in any situation.

Self is our worst enemy and satan is defeated. He can attack whomever he wants, but has to ask permission to do anything to God's people. The Lord allows circumstances in our lives to train us. Sickness, illness, and disease come from the pit of hell but God will allow it because He can fix anything and turn it around. Whatever Satan takes from us He will give it back in abundance. There is a lesson in all we go through; do not break your connection to God regardless of how you feel. Put your feelings behind you and stand strong. I do know it's not what we go through but how we go through. Selah!

Yeshua had a problem with His family. They did not believe who He said He was. I have the same problem. Years ago He told me to tell my family who I was in Him. I certainly became the black sheep of the family with how I was mistreated. The reason could be jealousy. Satan is jealous. Whatever the reason, Yeshua did not want my sister to be part of it any longer. Through me, He gave her that word more than once. I believe He wanted to use her to change the minds of others. When she told me she did not want me at her house anymore. I did not say anything. I left and started hanging out at the Clifton Library. Sitting in the park by the pond; trying to catch a breeze off the water on hot summer days; is where you could find me. I tried to hide the tears that filled my eyes every time I thought of what was taking place. I stayed until dark then had to figure out where to go from there because it was not time to go to my son's house. I was not going to sit in the park after dark.

I was lying on the floor praying when I heard laughter in the heavens. The Lord said, "Satan asked to speak to you personally." I asked, what was that about? "He thinks you want to converse with him," What do you say? I asked. "Talk to him, it can not hurt." And say what? I do not want to talk to him! "Just do it for me!" He said. It was a very hot day at the 100-degree mark. I decided to stay in and study the Bible. Sitting on the bed with my back against the headboard I was surrounded by the Bible, two study bibles, a concordance, a notepad, and a pen. The headboard was up against the window. The sun shone so bright over my shoulder that I did not need to turn on the light. I was writing and did not realize the room had become dark. I turned to look out of the window and then looked at the time. It's high noon. Why is it so dark? Are we going to have a storm? I said to myself.

All of a sudden a stench came across my nose. I could not take it on an empty stomach. I almost regurgitated right there in the bed. The scent got stronger and stronger. I yelled, Oh Lord! with my hand over my mouth. Then my stomach began to settle. I looked up and saw a gray mist in the doorway of my room; no particular shape, just a cloud-like figure moving like a soft wind was blowing. Satan called my name and said, I love you. He said it again. I ignored him and went back to writing hoping he would leave. Somehow I could see in the dark. Time had passed and he was still in the doorway. I asked, are you still here? What is it that you want with me? He asked if I loved him. I love you, he said.

I know you did not come here to ask that question! There has to be another reason, I said. I rebuke you because the Father rebukes you. As I held up the pointer finger of my right hand waving it back and forth, I proceeded to let him have it. Stay out of my life! Stay out of my relationship with Christ! Stay out of my children's lives, my grandchildren's lives, my family's lives! You have no authority here. I spoke very fast then put my finger down and went back to writing. The figure stood in the doorway for another forty-five minutes or so. I knew he left when the scent was getting fainter. Goodbye! The Lord laughed and said, "Oh he does not want to mess with you." The test continues. From that point, the evil in my life became stronger. I could tell it was because I met with the evil one.

There were three times in total that I met with him face to face. Satan was trying to pull me out of God's hands using my family as bait. Everyone is suffering from sickness and disease but they do not know why. I was called some ungodly names, had things thrown at me, lies told about me, and talked about right in front of my face as if my existence did not matter. Of course, those things were happening already but were now more profound. I am hurt watching this but I am not giving up on God. Satan can not get me that easily. I know God was taking me through the fire preparing me for the last days.

The Lord revealed to me that I was elevated to the Mercy Seat. My knowledge of what happens there was fragmented. He began to enlighten me. "You no longer strive to reach this place. You have an opening over you connected to the heavens. Just ask and you shall receive. Watch what you ask for, it will manifest. You do not have to pray, yell, or cry, just ask and I will answer you. Divine protection, ArchAngel Michael, will be with you everywhere you go." As His voice resonated through my body tears ran down my face. What a feeling to know God loves me even though I took Him through hard times during my journey. We can get to a place where He defines us as righteous. I never call myself righteous because I still sin against Him. I am a sinner saved by God's amazing grace who repents daily.

It was after that connection with the Lord that my spirit was taken up. As I lay down on my back I felt my spirit leave my body. I thought it was a dream but I had just gotten into bed. The tiredness was leaving and my eyes were closing on my way to dreamland. It was funny because I thought of the movie "Peter Pan." I have not seen that movie in decades. I was floating in the sky with nothing in sight but clouds until I came upon a huge white throne where the Lord was sitting. I said, excuse me, Your Highness, in a playful voice, why are you sitting like that in that fabulous chair? He was wearing a long white robe with a red rope tied around His waist and a red sash around His neck. His head was leaning against His fist. "I am waiting for my people," He said. Waiting on them to do what? I asked. He replied, "To get right." "You will tell them what to do to get right." Me? "Yes. I chose you," he said. I was immediately back in my body. I felt myself leaving, but returning I was just back and did not feel anything. The next morning I tried to remember what occurred. Was it a dream? It did ot feel like a dream. I remembered the Peter Pan comment and chuckled at the idea of thinking about a kiddie movie from my youth. It was in one of those heavenly sessions of my spirit leaving my body that He told me who to pray for and how to pray to cover them.

He told me if I fall, everyone I pray for will fall. I had to stay in line and be obedient for everyone else's sake. Having an intercessor standing in the gap does not mean people won't sin; it means the Lord will continue to work in their lives and not harden their hearts. Standing in the gap is when you put your foot in the door to keep it ajar. The door will not close and no one will be left behind. Amazingly, the Lord sees to it that everyone is covered by prayer. Those who do not know Him, those who do not want to know Him, and those who think they can live life without Him are all being prayed for. He leaves no one out. There are things we must do ourselves. The Lord waits patiently for us to do our part so He can move. There were seven times in total the Lord called my spirit to heaven for instruction. One does not have to be doing something special or be famous to be used by God. Every person born on earth has a job to do for Him. Ask what that is in prayer.

My car held out for a long time. When it continued to break down I gave it up. My son had his automobile to contend with. I appreciated it and was thankful for it. Now I had to get out of the house and walk for exercise. I made it a ritual to go in a different direction every time I went out. Some days I would head toward Totowa. I would walk up Union Avenue to Highway 46 by Forman Mills Warehouse and walk back. Some days I walk south through downtown Paterson up Main Street through Clifton into Passaic and back. Some days I walked from the west side to the north side into Haledon. On other days I went through downtown then east up Market Street to Route 80. One day I walked through downtown Paterson, into Clifton which is shaped like a "U". Then through Passaic to the other side of Clifton by Route 3. This is where I saw a housing development and decided I wanted to live there. I saw a strip mall right across the street which housed a movie theater, a laundry mat, a market, a bistro, a bakery, and more. I would not have to drive anywhere if I didn't want to. Dusk was falling and I had to get back. I knew I had gone too far when I had to push myself to keep going. If I stopped I would have to call my son to pick me up. I stayed in prayer. When I reached Paterson there was a blackout. I stopped on the corner of Main and Market streets. There was light up until that point. I went left down Market Street which was in total darkness. There was light in Burger King's parking lot four blocks down that helped me find my way. Up around Paterson Falls was pitch black. As the light from Burger King faded I could not tell if there were people or animals out there. The headlights of the passing cars gave light. I turned around to see what or who was around me each time an automobile passed by. It was also hard to know where the curb was to cross the streets. The lights passing by helped with that also.

I finally came upon the street where my son lives. His street was lit up like a hot summer's day in July. Okay, I thought, someone was playing a joke on me. I looked into the sky but there was no hint that anyone heard me. I was glad to shut the door behind me where I felt safe. I asked my son if he knew there was a blackout. He had no idea. He could not believe I walked in it. I had to walk. I did not want to call him asking for a ride. My Family said I wanted to mooch off people because I lived with him. They did not believe it was God who sent me there. He has not given me any word for them to know it was Him so they do not believe. I wanted to move more than they wanted me to go. A place of my own is what I asked for. The Lord was not feeling it. "Just do as you are told," He said.

My son's girlfriend joined in to create more of a hostile environment. She brought her young daughter and a couple of cousins over while he was at work. They ran back and forth around the house screaming. They jumped up and down on the furniture, knocking things over. I was not picking anything up. I came out of the room to see where she was. I looked out the window. Her car was not in sight. She opened the door, let them in, and left. I was not staying there. I was not babysitting. They tore the place up. When I returned my bed was broken. She would come into the house with an attitude, follow me around then call him telling him everything I was doing. He yelled and screamed for me to get out. On the other hand, Christ Yeshua kept telling me I better be obedient and stay where He assigned me. With everything that happened He said, "This is for you!" I was oblivious to what He meant. I did not understand but knew there would be a severe penalty if I left on my own accord. Yeshua said I would not survive the punishment that would come upon me. There was nothing good going on inside the house or outside the house as far as I was concerned. Things were getting worse, not better. I was between a rock and a hard place with no way out. I could not wait to get my first Social Security check which was coming up in a couple of years. With my first check, I intended to begin to pay my son back for all he had done, because I was grateful not to be out on the street all this time.

My sister with diabetes was taken to the hospital once again. It was pretty bad this time so my niece and I went together. We exited the elevator on her floor. There was a large group of doctors huddling and talking between the nurse's station and my sister's room. We made our way through them since none of them thought to step aside. How rude I thought. Her door was closed. We didn't think anything of it since there was so much noise outside her room. The nurse's station full of nurses was stationed right in front of her door. No one said anything to us as I turned the knob and went inside. My niece followed. We were shocked by the pile of ashes that were in the spot where my sister lay. Stunned, we could not move. I sent my niece to get the nurse.

As I stood there looking at the situation before my eyes I grew angry. How long was she lying here like this? No one thought to call her daughter! The nurse said she would be in shortly, she said as the door closed behind her. My niece walked to the foot of the bed and broke down crying. I walked over to the bed, laid my hands on the pile of ashes, and bellowed, I rebuke you, death angel! Satan, you can not have this life! Immediately my sister's form came to life. She opened her eyes and said, Oh, I didn't hear you come in Glo. My niece could not catch her breath. She started jumping and praising God. Her mother kept asking what was the matter. I explained and she kept thanking me. I said thank God it was Him, not me.

God showed Himself mighty and glorious that day not only to us but the hospital staff who just stood out there doing nothing. The nurse nor any doctor entered the room. We stayed a long time with the door closed talking. No one came in the room the whole time we were there, not even anyone authorized to take vitals. I guess they figured they would allow us time to mourn. They were truly surprised when we walked out of the room laughing and my niece asked them to call the kitchen because her mother was hungry. The nurse's eyes were big. She said, what! She repeated, my mother wants something to eat and drink. We had to leave. This was a Christian hospital and no one addressed the problem. No one said anything to us as we walked passed the station full of nurses and doctors. A couple of days later they discharged her. Do not play with God! He is not a force to be reckoned with. He is the highest Sovereign entity. Give Him glory!

Months later my niece called to say her mother was back in the hospital. She had called her two brothers to go with her and was waiting for them. I told her I had to go to Wayne, NJ to get a document and would stop at the hospital on my way back. As the bus approached the hospital the Lord told me to get off at this stop. I said I was going to pick up some paperwork and I would come back and stay here the rest of the day. He said in a stern voice, "I said get off here!" I was not happy but I stepped out of the bus and went inside. I had to wait two hours in the lobby before visiting her floor. I could have been back by then but there was nothing I could do. I had to wait.

The nurse stopped me from entering my sister's room in the ICU. She told me what medication she had just given her. As soon as I laid my things down on the chair the Lord spoke telling me to pray for her. Her back was to me. I took her left hand in my left hand then gently placed my right hand on her head because I thought she was asleep. Just as I went to pray, He said, "Pray to open the gates to receive her." I swung around and said, What! My sister said what's the matter? I told her not to worry. I was talking to the Lord. I communicated in my head saying, I'm not doing that! Tears began to fall. I could not keep my composure. Tell me you did not bring me here and spring this on me. He said, "Do it or I won't take her!" I positioned myself again. Abba! I called. The Holy Spirit leaned over me and began to pray. Knowing that it was my voice He was using I listened as He asked for the gates of heaven to be opened to receive her soul. I was speechless. She turned to say something. I cut her off, do not say anything, just rest. I will see you when I get there. He commanded me to leave. I took my things and walked out.

A few minutes later my niece texted me. We're here! Where? I text back. At the hospital. I just came out, I said. I didn't see you guys. I'm standing out front at the bus stop. She waved at me through the window pane. I boarded the bus. It wasn't long before she called and said her mother passed. Was she awake when you arrived, I asked. Yes, it was like she waited for us to get here, she said. Did she say anything? I asked. She was trying to say something but we could not understand her. They all said their goodbye's then the oldest brother said to her, do not say anything, just rest. We will see you when we get there. My sister was gone. I thought, my God is amazing! He is so good at what He does.

It was thirteen years and some months later that I was finally old enough to receive Social Security. The first installment was like pouring honey on pancakes. I felt so light I could have skipped all over town. I never grinned so much in all my life. Back when I filled out the paperwork the Lord told me not to accept the money. He said He would take care of me. I did think about it but went ahead with the process. Giving up everything and living on people had me in a state of mind thinking what would He do next! If He did not want me to have it He would have to stop the process himself.

It is hard living with other adults. I could not take it any longer even if it was a test. Yes, I admit I was disobedient. I offered my son money before doing anything. Even though the Bible says we must take care of our family no one had to take care of me. I was young enough to work and had no physical barriers that hindered me. My son was not taking any money from me. He gave an emphatic no! The Lord took me out of work and insisted I not go back. People do not believe or understand that it was God. We all have to suffer on this earth, this was part of my suffering. He does what He wants whenever He wants. He is Sovereign. Anything is possible with Him. Nothing is impossible. Our job is to be obedient.

I asked my daughter to take me to the housing development I saw on one of my excursions in Clifton, NJ. I made an appointment to view a studio apartment. We entered the office and there were three other people to view apartments. The woman took us to an area where they had a studio, one-bedroom, and two-bedroom apartments empty for viewing. The one bedroom was appealing but I could not afford it. On the way back to the office I was asked if I wanted to see the actual apartment I would get. Then she said it's identical to the one you saw. The only difference is that it is on the first floor like you wanted. I declined. The day I went to take window coverings and products to clean before moving in surprised me. A huge pile of dirt was on the sidewalk right in front of the stairs. I went around it and stepped up from the side of the porch to open the front door. There were two rooms on the first floor and two on the second. My studio was behind the staircase on the first floor. The hallway was dirty and smelled like someone peed on the floor for seven days straight. Going into my apartment the doorknob felt sticky. I began cleaning right away after washing my hands and putting on gloves. For a studio it was big, It reminded me of a tiny house. The kitchen and bathroom were not in the main room but had their own spaces. Surprisingly there was a lot of storage space. I loved it. I thought It was just right for me then noticed it was not symmetrical to the one I was shown. The lady was not telling the truth.

I ordered a U-haul truck and asked my other two sons to help me move. They hung the curtains and set up the twin bed my sister gave me along with a table and two stools. Downsizing was inevitable. I gave my bedroom set away and called a second-hand store to pick up some boxes I donated. After my sons left, I sat on the bed waiting for the sofa bed to be delivered. The following day a foul smell swept past our noses as my daughter and I stepped into the hallway returning from food shopping. The atmosphere was full of that horrific odor. My daughter, who was an EMT, said it smelled like someone was sick and was taking medication. We covered our noses and mouths. I ran to get the Lysol and sprayed it outside my door.

After everything was put away I grabbed some gloves and went to clean the hall. I left the outside door open while I cleaned the walls, stairs, banister, and the floor. The whole place smelled of bleach and Lysol Disinfectant when I got through. The only tenant that was home was the man upstairs over me. He was not pleased. He came out of the apartment to approach me saying, the maintenance man cleans the hall. Well, I said, he should be fired because this hall was filthy. I guess we can count on you to clean, he said. We both laughed. I laughed to keep from blowing my top. I guess he laughed because he could see I was trying to hold it back with the side-eye look I gave him. I went inside to wash up, change my clothes and rest. I liked the place. I saw myself being there for a long time.

The same neighbor knocked on my door to tell me he had bed bugs. He asked if I saw the man who lived across the hall from me. No, you are the only one I've seen and spoken to. You do know there are three men in this building? I just heard it from you. I asked if they had bed bugs too. He pointed to my neighbor's door across the hall and said, oh yeah, she has them she does not clean. Okay, I get the hint they are all homosexuals. He was telling me they did not want me here. He asked if the office called me. I said no. He said they are supposed to notify you concerning pests. Thanks for telling me. I called the office with an attitude. Are you telling me you knew the three other apartments in this building are infested with bed bugs and you rented to me anyhow? They called the exterminator post haste. While waiting for pest control, I noticed a space between the baseboard and the wall. When he arrived the exterminator asked if I had bed bugs. I do not know what they look like and showed him the spaces in the baseboard. If I do, they could have come in through there, I said. But I have not seen anything unusual. Looking around he did not see any bugs. He said I won't work down here. I will treat them upstairs where they are alive. I was the one who called; yes, you will treat my apartment also.

He explains how they are not like roaches and other bugs. I did not want to hear it. To make me feel comfortable he treated my place this time but had to come back a few more times for the other apartments. I went to the store and bought stuff to kill bed bugs. I sprayed my furniture and vacuumed the couch. I mixed Boric Acid and sugar with a little water to make a paste and put it all around the baseboard and in every hole I saw. Before it dried I sprinkled the dry mixture on top of the moist. I moped the floor every day. I wanted assurance as he treated the apartments around me.

Taken hostage by a huge snowstorm right after I moved in allowed me to see how I felt about living in the apartment. I loved it. A few days later the streets and sidewalks were clean but some snow was still on the grass area. I heard someone call my name and looked out of the curtain. My upstairs neighbor was standing there in black stiletto heels, a black pencil skirt, and a white blouse with a wig on his head. I stood there with my arms folded across my chest leaning on the window frame looking him up and down, I opened the window and said that outfit is banging! He smiled and said thanks. From that point on we began having friendly talks. He started calling me Glor. I guess I was accepted. I continued to spray the hall, especially the banister and doorknobs.

Sitting comfortably snuggled in the corner of the couch, reading a book, Yeshua said, "I need you to go somewhere, get up and get dressed." I showered, did my hair, and got dressed. The bus stop was a few feet from my door but I did not know how much change I had. I gathered it all, swept it into my pocket, and headed out the door. I asked where am I going? He answered, "Paterson." I had enough change to get there and back so there was no problem. As the bus pulled into the Paterson Bus Terminal I asked where to? He said, "I want you to go up to a pastor's house." The pastor had a big house in the Eastside Park area and used his living room as the sanctuary.

The pastor and his wife were standing near the door as I entered. They were surprised to see me and asked why I was there. The Lord never told me why I was there and since I did not hear his voice, I said with a smile, I came to the festivities. They both said in unison festivities! I laughed and said, or whatever and walked in and took a seat. The room started filling up. I got the idea that someone was going to give a speech because a few men were sitting in chairs at the front of the room. After the pastor prayed one man stood and introduced himself and his colleagues stating they were representing a Christian College in Newark, NJ. Leaflets were passed to all who attended. Mine was presented with a little hesitation. When I opened it there was information about the college with an application. I listened to what was being said with no idea I would sign up until I heard, "I want you to apply!" I must learn to focus on my facial expressions to control them. I immediately looked up and all eyes were on me.

I felt my eyes bulging and my lips were pressed firmly together as I screamed, in my head, no! I'm not doing this! The Lord said, "Do it for me." I asked how I would be doing it for him when I have to do the work? He said, "I will help you." I fall for that line every time. He always showed me I could do it without his help by not helping. Needless to say, I filled out the application. Finishing college after my children were all out of school was my goal originally. The Lord kept holding it off and at sixty-seven years old wanted me to go back. I've been bamboozled again.

†

CHAPTER XII

NOT FOR MYSELF

Waiting for the semester to start I applied for grants and scholarships. New students were called in to fill out forms. One woman asked if this was the paperwork for the two-year course they were advocating called the Lead Program. I said I applied for the two-year speed course also. Then one after another the other women chimed in. The two men had authoritative positions at the college and neither one had any idea of a two-year speed course. They were going to check on it for us. We were told to fill out the paperwork we had so that if there was no speed course we would not have to wait another semester to start school. A red flag went up. I was a little leary and thought about chucking the whole thing. With a little encouragement from the rest of the women, I filled out the schedules. I had to take the entry test while I was there because I had not done it yet. I was not prepared in the least. It was unexpected and pretty easy to get through. They were pleased with my score.

The year 2014 was when I began busing to Newark, NJ to attend college. With a bookbag on my back, a pep in my step, and a smile on my face I was important that day. It felt good. To be honest I was a little concerned about the age factor, and was not alone. I recall how the other matriarchs expressed their concerns when we filled out our first schedules. This is God's school filled with His people; what could go wrong? On the first day, I felt so disrespected. Never before have I seen such dirty looks. Sneers from professors and faculty members was disheartening. A position someone holds should never permit them to be nasty to others. I am positive the restriction policies of this establishment forbid discrimination.

These people are breaking the code of conduct, and the laws of God. In His word, the Holy Bible commands us to love Him with all our heart, soul, and mind. It also says to love your neighbor as you do yourself {Mark 12:30,31}. When we express love it means we received him in our hearts because He is love. There was no proof of that here. My people were the worst, turning the corners of their mouths down and turning their noses up. If they only knew what they looked like to me at that moment. I felt as if they would dare speak, they would probably ask what was I doing there! When I went into prayer, I said, Lord, please do not let me treat anyone like this. They know nothing about me. If getting a degree makes people act like they are superior, I do not want it. Go before me Lord, make my path straight. My day went well in spite of it all. Lord, I thank you for your grace.

The next day four female matriarchs were getting off the elevator as I was getting on. They greeted me and asked when I started classes. I told them about the reception I received. They all responded with the same reaction, the same thing happened to us! One of the ladies said, and they say this is a Christian school. I agreed with her, yes! Pray about it, they said, and went on their way. These young ladies were all in the graduating class. I never saw them again. The disrespect did not stop but continued daily. Teaching senior citizens might be challenging in some instances but it goes along with the job. That is what teachers, professors, and trainers signed up to do. Look around! Your feet still tread the same ground mine does. No one has risen above humanity. I see why God calls for us to be humble. Our heads swell. We think more of ourselves than we ought to think. God sees it all. Lord have mercy on us!

It was evident a professor of color did not want to address me when I walked into her office for help. She turned her back to me and was quick to interrupt as I spoke and answered something I did not ask. Then she yelled at me. I was enraged. How dare she! I can't tell you what I felt like doing at that moment but took a couple of deep breaths instead. She walked to her desk. I explained what I needed from the table where I was sitting. She looked up and then said, oh! Right then I thought how could prideful, judgemental, prejudiced people of God teach and lead others? This behavior is unacceptable. I wonder if Yeshua ever chastised them for their actions. The Bible instructs us on how believers should act toward one another. This is a prime example of why it can not be enforced. God's people are not living righteously.

During my stay I met some anointed students and staff members. Mass at midday was lit. We went back to class joyfully singing praise. After class one of my schoolmates had a headache. She was telling me how it was pounding. I had books in my hand and my coat hanging over my arm so I said let's go in this room. I put my things down and told her to have a seat. Both my hands were on her temples as I commanded healing. I picked my things up and told her I had to go. In amazement, she said it's gone! Yes, I said it only takes a second. The anointing of the Holy Spirit works immediately. We went through that a few times. I told her to cut down on some of the daily activities that were stressing her out. Others heard about it and came to me to pray for them or lay hands on them. I didn't mind. It was God's work. It's His power I can not heal a soul without Him. From the very beginning when He told me to get up and go I never thought it was for me. I was on assignment. He had work for me to do here. I loved the whole ambiance of the college scene. I did not like those who thought they had acquired something that no one else could achieve. God says each one, teach one. When we teach others what we know then we are on one accord.

A haughty attitude is pride. It is a sin that is alive and dwells in the hearts of many Christians. "Haughtiness is blatant and disdainful pridefulness, having or showing an attitude of superiority and contempt for people or things perceived to be inferior" [Mirriam Webster]. Church, the reality is we must conform to those things listed above, not just study them. God's expectation of human beings is to be obedient to His will and His way. He is not filled with joy when a Christian brother or sister plots against one another. We do not have to look alike or do things alike, just treat each other right. Every time that prideful spirit comes my way I pray for those who entertain it. There is no room for witchcraft in my life.

It was time to fill out the coming semester's schedule. As I counted credits I knew something was wrong. A group of us gathered together the next day and figured out the count was off because we were not taking the accelerated course. I was disappointed and went to speak with someone in charge. She was knowledgeable and explained everything even if it was not her particular field. I was told as soon as they could get enough students to fill a class I would be called. My first thought was to give up right then. Some of the students said it doesn't make sense to quit because we are already here. They were right but most of them were not my age. They were not aware of what I went through with the Lord concerning school. For years I asked the Lord if I could go back to school. He would answer, "Not yet." It took so long that the yearning left. He waited until I was over it and did not want to do it anymore. Then He commanded me to go to see if I would be obedient. I could walk away but instead, I said yes, call me, please. It was not long before the class came together and I am glad I stayed.

The LEAD Program is made up of small groups of people which are called cohorts. "Students can earn a Bachelor's Degree by converting their life experiences and prior learning assessments that can translate into 30 credits. Eligibility consisted of having completed approximately 48 hours from an accredited institution of higher learning, and a GPA of 2.0 or higher" [Pillar College 2001]. It allows a student to get four years of learning in half the time. I loved it. School was a lot of work and a lot of reading. The amount of homework was ridiculous but enlightening. Except for three women, all of the students in my cohort were pastors or jr. pastors. Most of the professors were knowledgeable and qualified pastors who taught at a fast pace. I could stay in the program for four years and still love it.

Truly the Holy Spirit visited that school through employees, administrators, educators, and students. Praise and worship lifted my spirit and helped me get through. I confess I could have done a better job. I was angry at God for waiting so long to send me back. The cost of college today is off the scale. It is a challenge to live without higher learning striving to make ends meet, and a harder challenge to live after college trying to finance it. People will need a higher paying job, or two with trying to delegate payments to make things work. I am thinking about loan repayment which starts before school ends; I had to start setting money aside before then. I would highly suggest Trade School to anyone interested in higher learning unless their goals warrant a college degree. With the certification and a couple of college courses, one can surely move up the corporate ladder. Paying for college was an issue for me.

I applied for grants and used part of my 401K Plan. What was left of my savings, Yeshua commanded me to rebuild a small orphanage in Nigeria, Africa that had burned down. I was reluctant because I would not have any money at all. But I had to be obedient. The Lord gave me the person's name, and telephone number and told me to call to let him know the money was coming. This keeper of the house had been crying out to the Lord to help the children. When I called the man kept asking who are you? Again I repeated my name and then added from the United States. Jesus gave me your name and number. I am to send you money to rebuild the orphanage as soon as you tell me where to and how to send it. What! He screamed. Who told you to call? He was in shock. He could not believe what was happening. He asked me to repeat everything as he handed the phone to a female. I could hear him screaming and praising, thanking Jesus in the background. She told me to send the money through Western Union. Fortunately, there was one across the street from me in the mall. In less than half an hour I called to let them know it was ready to be picked up. He asked if I was on social media. I said yes. He sent photos to my page of the fire and a group photo of all the children saying thank you. I tell you this story to tell you God knows what He is doing. He said He would pay back everything I spent. He has it all figured out. He needs our obedience to get His work done. We are His mouthpiece, His hands, and His feet. He wanted to bless this man, house the children, and get the money out of my hands. Whatever He does there are many facets to it.

After I sent the money I had nothing left. I could not pay the rent. I used some of my 401K account money to pay the rent each month because my social security check did not cover it in total. The housing development would not accept partial payments. I cried out to the Lord begging for the rent to be paid. Finally, I received a letter from the housing development stating I had to leave. I heard a word from heaven clear and plain as day. "You do not have to leave. I am going to take care of it." I waited to see what He had in mind to do. The next payment was due and I heard nothing from the Lord. I waited until the grace period to contact the office and was fined again for not paying the rent a second time. I received another letter stating that I must leave now. My nerves were shattered especially from the court visit that was embarrassing and belittling. I kept living and going to school as if nothing happened. No one knew what I was going through, I just waited on the Lord.

There was a knock at the door one morning. For the second time a Constable stood with an eviction notice in his hand looking at me in wonder. Why are you still here? he asked. Looking around he said it looks like you do not intend to go. I did not offer the information that the Lord said I did not have to pack because I was not going anywhere. He went on, you received a letter that you had to leave. I didn't want to do this, he said as he threw his hands up. I went on vacation for two weeks to give you time to vacate. Tears were rolling down my face. I could not say anything. He was right. I was listening for the voice of the Lord to tell me what to do in this situation. I heard nothing. It was a good thing I had already showered and got dressed. I had to take only what was necessary. As I walked out the door he immediately changed the lock. The Constable stared at me with a sad face as he drove past.

The weather forecast that day was a rainstorm that happened to start as I sat down on a bench outside the complex. Sitting in the rain that masked my tears I looked up and told the Lord He reneged on His promise. I was done. I had no money and was put out on the street. I did not want to go any further with His plan. My complaining was interrupted when the wind began to blow. I could not breathe. The rain came down so hard that I took cover in the laundromat across the street. He finally told me to call my pastor. For what! I asked. What can she do? I am not calling anyone; you did this, I said. This was your plan to have me evicted all along. "Call her!" He said. The pastor sent her granddaughter in the pouring rain to get me. I didn't know what to tell them except I had nowhere to go. It took them by surprise like it did me. He put them in a position to make immediate decisions. I remember when the pastor and her husband wanted to purchase a condo in the building where they lived. They asked me to pray for God to make it possible; I did. Then they asked me to bless the apartment before they moved in. Here I am standing in the center of their condo without a place to lay my head asking if I could stay until I heard from the Lord. I knew it was him who sent me; I did not know why.

They were kind enough to give this a chance. I could hear whispers coming from the other room where she and her family gathered. I sat in the living room alone with my head in my hands crying. I know in my heart this experience is linked to receiving what He said my family and I would possess in my obedience to Him. It is hard to always be obedient trying to follow Him and do not know what He is doing next. I walked away from a situation like this; Yeshua put me right back in it again. "Led like a lamb to the slaughter" {Isaiah 53:7}. This is how He wants me to go. From the start, I told Him I could not do it and yet there is a sense of letdown every time this happens.

The pastor's family rallied together daily. Her house was always full of people which made it impossible to study or do homework. I went down to the community room where I could work. There was no one in there so I set my books down. The super, who is the pastor's husband, came in and asked how I got in. I said the door was unlocked and the lights were on. He said the door was supposed to be locked at all times if not in use and I was not supposed to be in there. I packed up my bookbag without saying a word, slung it over my back, and headed downtown to catch the bus to Newark where I completed my work in the computer room. I had a lot of work to finish. It was dark when I returned. They asked me where I was and I told them at the school. They could not believe I went all the way to Newark. On days I had class I arose early, took a shower, and left by 6:45 am. On all other days, I helped keep the house clean, helped with the children in her nursery, and helped clean the building's hallways, stairs, and community room. I also helped her go food shopping.

One day after school I rang the bell to be buzzed in. I kept ringing the buzzer but no one would answer. A neighbor came out of the door and I went in taking the stairs. Just as I approached the door to the apartment I overheard talk concerning me. A voice from inside the apartment said do not open the door, leave her out there. At that moment I decided to leave and did not care where I went. I knocked. When the door opened the pastor's husband, a granddaughter, and other family members were there. It was quiet. I said thanks. The stay was not all good but it kept me off the street which I thought was God's purpose. Later they told me they thought I was sent there to be persecuted. Maybe so, that is how God works. I know we have to be servants and are used in other people's walks to bring us to our highest potential in God, but I was not going to pay anyone to persecute me. I had to go.

Early one morning when I left the pastor's house, it was dark because the sun had not yet peeked its head over the horizon. I began walking down one block to Straight Street then turned left and headed toward

Broadway. I was wearing black sandals, jean stretch pants, and a black top, with my hair in an afro and a book bag draped over my shoulders. From the back, I could be mistaken for a teen on their way to school, especially because I am of short stature. I saw the headlights of a car on the ground coming from behind me that crossed over to my side of the street. I turned to the right to see who it was. A Hispanic man driving with his window down about to say something looked in my eyes and started rolling the window up. A thought came to me that this is how people are snatched up and trafficked.

The Holy Spirit took control and the car began to zig zag back and forth from one side of the street to the other. It missed the post holding up the trestle in front of us and went up on the sidewalk. Still, in the zig-zag pattern, the car turned into the warehouse parking lot, made a U-turn, and came back out again. Then crossed the street to make another turn, never touching the wall in front of it. This happened four times. On the last exit from the lot the car made a left turn and sped up Straight Street at about ninety miles an hour. It happened quickly, only taking a couple of minutes as I stood watching from the curb. Then I heard the voice of the Lord saying, "This is the protection that is over you." I thanked him and said, I pray for all who are abducted this way. When I got back to the house I told everyone what took place that morning.

I never sat under a pastor or prophet who spoke into my life concerning the future. It was 1975 when the Lord prophesied over me. He told me how my story would end although the lengths to what I had to go through to get there were omitted. He said my family would rise to prestigious positions, some would have fame and fortune, some would be entrepreneurs, and become homeowners, and I would be rich and able to supply all their needs. That was only part of all He said. For this to happen I had to give up everything because He chose me to hold a place in heaven for my family. They were skeptical and since years passed and nothing happened they say I was lying. I have been living with other people since 1999 unable to afford a place of my own. Any money that comes into my hands I am instructed what to do with it. I can only spend what is necessary on myself. I pay the amount Yeshua suggests to the people who take me in. I purchase my food and personal items, do my laundry, help clean the house, and do other chores. The Holy Bible says to count it all joy for He is testing my faith [James 1:2-4]. I do not know about joy but I am grateful. However, I still walk in my depression wishing it were all over.

If you want to know a person, live with them. This will bring out feelings deep within the soul they did not know they had. You're looked at as if your life now belongs to them. In their minds, they are in authority over you. Cinderella or Little Orphan Annie syndrome kicks in. Clean my house; strip the grease from my stove; vacuum the furniture and shampoo the carpet are the commands. I learned as a teenager these are things people have not attempted to do for years, and now can pass them over to you. They are insensitive to your situation and what you have to endure. Yeshua said to cook and clean for my keep along with a small fee. I am not cooking unless it's for myself. Women do not want anyone taking over their kitchen. I do believe in cleaning the house and doing chores. I know when I am not wanted and how to keep out of everyone's way. I feel out of place in other people's houses as if I am taking up space that someone could be utilizing. But I won't be blatantly abused. If God is sending someone into your home it is blessed and everyone who dwells there will be blessed. Christians should know this. The whole ordeal could be a test of how we treat others. If you are fair He will repay it. Please understand God was taking me through humbling experiences among other things. He was testing me, burning me with fire, and working with all who were involved at the same time. Nothing is one-sided with him. He does a mighty work that purifies. He will work with you until you are like pure gold.

My daughters were looking for me and figured I must be with the pastor and came to find out for themselves. They wanted to know why I did not tell them about the eviction. We talked for a few minutes. I said I was leaving here but didn't know where I was going. One of them said she had an extra bedroom with a bed. I ordered a mattress and waited two days for delivery then said my goodbyes. I stayed at the pastor's house for five months in total.

✝

C H A P T E R X I I I

CONTINUING MY MISSION

2016 is the year I moved in with my daughter who lived alone in a two-bedroom apartment in Saddle Brook, NJ. It was a nice area. The grounds were manicured and beautiful to look at, yet people are the same everywhere you go. There was no way I could sleep at night with the window open. The weed smoking in the back of our building was out of control. There was no backyard but there was a dog walk so people were back there constantly. The first thing I did was find out how to get to school. The next day of class I headed in that direction. Two weeks after moving in I had to go into the office to put my name on the lease. The Lord said, "Only answer the questions asked of you, don't offer anything else." The woman interviewing me was condescending and insulting. I sat and looked at her while she spewed bile from her mouth. When she asked a question between insults I answered them briefly. There was a problem while entering my information into the system. She kept asking the same questions over and over. I asked if there was a problem. She says I have to call the head office for instructions. I did not offer a response. They tried different techniques to get the system to work but settled on putting my name in with zero income. I was told that was the only way the system would accept my name. Therefore, I could not be charged anything and my daughter's rent would stay the same. Look at God! He is good!

The complex is right off Market Street which is a main thoroughfare in that city. I walked around making myself familiar with the neighborhood. My doctor's office and bank were directly across the street. Every type of store you could think of was within four blocks of walking distance of the apartment. Just like Clifton, I did not need an automobile. God makes it convenient for me but Satan is always in the picture. People will comment on my situation without looking at their own messed up lives. One day in the laundromat a white woman asked why would I want to live with my daughter. I replied, excuse me? She went on; I do not know why anyone would want to live with their kids after they left home. I looked her in her eyes and added, I do not want to live with my children, but I figured she lived under my roof for thirty years so as far as I am concerned I have some catching up to do. That's one way to look at it, she said. People need to take a step back and mind their own business. They do not know what God is doing.

My son came over to say he and one of my grandsons were on their way to get my belongings from the housing complex where I was evicted. He wanted me to go with him. I declined. I was working on three essays, two papers, and homework that had to be in by that Monday. My children discussed the issue without my input. He decided to go after work to see what he could do. They told him yes he could get my things, but get it quickly. I said throw the furniture in the dumpsters in the back of the building. All I wanted was my clothes and books. After getting my work done I called him to let him know I could help with the move. By the time my daughter picked me up and drove me there, they were just about finished. He was angry and spoke with an attitude, throwing and breaking my things. He should have not gone at all. If they had asked me they would have known I did not want the stuff.

No one touched my belongings that sat for five months, in a building, with other apartments that were infested. The day I went in for the walk through my daughter and I were the only people of color in the group. The woman who took us around to view the apartments gave a side-eyed look and a slight grin when I entered her office. My daughter and I looked at each other. She knew the building was bug-ridden and had three male tenants who did not clean. I knew the Lord was in control and knew all of what was happening. I left my son's house when He told me not to. The infestation and eviction were punishment for doing so. He allowed me to use that place until I finished school three and a half years later. At the time I was evicted, we were preparing to graduate.

I could do whatever He asked of me while in my own apartment, but

He is not in agreement with that. Anyway, I would have to save at least three times the rent needed to ensure it will be paid every month. Then I thought, I was evicted and no one would ever accept me with that on my record. In my bedroom, I spent 80% of my time doing homework, exercising, or sitting quietly on the bed or floor to think. I complain to God about the ongoing gossip about me because people do it in my face with boldness. The accusers think they are accurate in what they say without knowing the story. That is what upsets me the most. No one has ever come to me to ask me if anything was true. They just believe what they hear even if it's lies. I wonder how much was added to the basic story and how far outside of the family the stories traveled. God forgive them for they know not what they do.

As I stated previously, I was not in college for myself, but for those God had me reach. My cohort was an anointed one. While I was there I gave a word from God, laid hands on, helped, and prayed for others. God let them know He heard them and was about to make great strides in their lives. Some Professors prophesied in our classrooms. I was intrigued by the testimonies they shared. When you hear the background of others your own story doesn't sound so bad. We are all on a mission for God. The President of the school set up a meeting to inform us of some changes that had already taken place, and what was to come. Everyone was excited. About two weeks earlier my friends and I were sitting at the table in the lunchroom talking. I told them about some big changes that God was making at there. At the meeting, the President finished speaking and everyone was in awe of the progress. I asked the group if anyone remembered that I said the very same things word for word. The looks on their faces told the story when they recalled the day in question. They were even more impressed because they knew it was God and not me. He was targeting someone in the group. I did not know who.

Not everyone was impressed with who I am in Christ. It is Christians who are most offended. Some tried to discredit me the whole time I was in school. It is most disturbing to me that my family is still in disbelief. I experienced depression because of rejection from my family. Their mindset is such that I want to freeload and avoid work. There is nothing they have that I want. I want my own. My life has been filled with church hurt as well. I've been ostracized, persecuted, and cast out. We all have to go through things. I know the Lord wants to see if we would choose Him in our trials and valleys. Will we still love and praise Him; But be obedient above all? In our valley is when He teaches us. I must keep that in mind as He continues to send me to live with others. I know it's to bring about change in me. The closer we get to God the harder our walk gets. His training is intense.

I heard my daughter say she should call a carpet cleaning service. All second-floor apartments were carpeted. She saw spots that I didn't see. I thought it was a play on words and that was her way of telling me to do it. I ignored the statement and went into the bedroom which consisted of a single bed, a desk, and a closet. I kept thinking the carpet on the stairs did need cleaning. The bottom landing was dirty from stepping in from the outside. I saw a product in a magazine and ordered it. It showed how easy and in-depth the cleaning was in the end. I followed the instructions but did not realize it would involve so much of my strength. The instructions said light brushing. I had to use all my might with a scrub brush in hand. That's how dirty the section was. I felt a kink in the lower right side of my back so I thought to call it quits for now. I washed my hands and started preparing lunch. I could not reach the third shelf above my head so I stood on a stool. My arm was still too short so I gave it a little more stretch. At that moment I heard a crunching sound and could not move. I was stuck in place with my right arm resting on the shelf, my left hand holding onto the sink, while my tippy toes graced the stool underfoot. There was a pain in my right shoulder that stopped me every time I made an attempt to get down. I took deep breaths in through my nose and let them out slowly through my mouth which helped calm my nerves. When I felt secure I lowered my arm a little with each breath exhaled until it was at my side then jumped backward off the stool to the floor. That took hours.

Once my arm was in a downward position I could not lift it back up. I could only bend it from the elbow and keep it close to my body. The pain was excruciating! Oh well, I said. That's it for the clean carpet. The expression on my daughter's face was such that she did not believe me when I told her what occurred. The next day the carpet looked a little cleaner but needed a second scrub.

I found out pretty quickly there were a lot of things I could not do with one hand. Having a strong threshold for pain I did not seek medical treatment. I pushed it to the back of my mind to control it. They say what you do to one side of your body, do to the other side also to keep symmetry between the two sides working as one entity. I spent the next two weeks doing light exercises to stretch the left side of my body without harming it. This made me feel a little better and alleviated some of the pain. My daughter rushed in announcing that she bought a house and we had to move then asked where I was going. I ignored that question because if she had told me when she started looking for a house I could've made some kind of arrangements. I had to seek the Lord. Remember I was not living in her house on my own accord, but His. As usual, He did not respond. We went to Home Depot and came back with a car full of materials and began packing. The pain intensified from all the moving around, lifting, and folding. Even in my condition, I tried to help her with her packing. I made it down to one last bag that needed to be double-bagged. I could not do it. A pain shot from my lower back up to my right shoulder then across my back to my left shoulder that brought tears to my eyes. I sat down on the bed. The pain kept me tossing all night long. I wanted to give the movers some help the next day but thought I would save my energy to organize things at the new place.

The moving company was composed of three young black men just starting their entrepreneurship. My daughter thought she would help them by giving them her business. We gave them pointers on things they didn't know about handling other people's furniture, which should help them immensely. The movers sat everything in the living room which is the first room you enter from the front door. I grabbed my throw blanket, laid it on the floor, and put whatever I could not carry on it then pulled it into the bedroom. I used my forearms keeping my elbows pressed to my side, and my back straight to keep from using the shoulder. I put each thing where I wanted it as opposed to stacking them in a pile and then sorting them out later. By the time I was finished, my room was complete. The next day we finished putting all of the downstairs together. There are two bedrooms, a bathroom, a kitchen, a dining area, and a living room. Upstairs was her bedroom, a bathroom, and her office. The house is a blessing, however; it is not mine. Once again moving and never coming into my own.

From the outside, it looks like a quaint little house on a hill but the inside speaks volumes. It was beautifully renovated. I recall while living in

Saddle Brook the Lord asked me what kind of house I wanted. At the time a few of my grandchildren were going through some things and needed a place to live. I needed a four-bedroom house with two or more bathrooms and a basement so my grandchildren would have a home where we could all share the costs. Each one can save money over time to purchase their own. He never answered me. I didn't give any idea as to the layout of the rooms but as I looked around, this house had everything I asked for. I was confused. Wait a minute! I did not want my grandchildren in the street homeless but she got the house. He said, "Remember you gave everything up." He was not letting me forget that. What about my grandchildren? They still need help.

I was furious even though I did not know what He had planned. Do not get the wrong idea, even during the times when I am upset with the Lord I continue to repent, fast and lay prostrate in prayer at six in the morning for two and a half hours or more. My spirit may be low but I press on. My daughter found out her son needed a place to stay and immediately prepared a place for him. The Lord also helped the others find a place to live. I praised Him for shelter. My instruction was to stay where I was even though my grandson moved in. It has been many years of waiting for God to use me in my purpose in life. He constantly tells me, "I'm saving you for last." So the anticipation continues.

I read somewhere that exercise brings energy and lifts the spirit. Consequently, to take up some of my time, I implemented exercise into my everyday regimen. I used some of my fasting time from 12:00 am to 12:00 pm to fit prayer and an exercise schedule into the morning hours. I felt great, lost weight, and toned my body. I masked the depression deep within for a short while until it burst through like a spout spewing hazardous materials everywhere. When something weighs heavy on the mind the pressure of holding it down will bring action that reveals the worst in a person. How is it possible to feel the way I do as a child of God? Whenever I speak of what I do not like or what I do not want I walk right into it as a test. He has taken everything I want away from me and what I do not want is walking me through it.

When I left the city of Paterson, NJ, I vowed to myself and God that I would never come back, and then found myself right where I did not want to be. The Lord said to me, "Your words must speak life, not negativity."

"When I ask you to do something, be obedient. Do it whether you want to or not, lives depend on you. I will not be able to use you if you put your wants before mine. Your words send you down a path to show you I am in control." He opened my eyes to some things I was speaking into existence that were counterproductive. I get it! I have to think about what I want to say before actually speaking it into the atmosphere.

Time is speeding up. The closer we get to the end the quicker it will move. In the year 2024, I am still living with my daughter and her son since 2016. The Lord does not tell anyone He stationed me in their home but forbids me to go against His commands. The enemy has been working overtime to agitate me and get me to step out of the will of God to leave here. Through it all I have been teaching some about Yeshua and giving Bible Study to others. It has been going slow, one person at a time. He promises that it will turn around soon.

EPILOGUE

Stay Teachable; there is much to learn about what God is doing in these end times. He is releasing information and I am trying to receive it all. Study to make yourselves approved. When we do research He drops information in our spirit. Continue to pray for your family and Church because the enemy is attacking them, in these last days. The devil separates. God assembles. Yeshua does not wait until we are clean, He works through our mess to bring His plan to fruition. He will never leave you but will work with you until the end.

Allowing you to look into my life is to show that God uses everyone for the good and the bad, whether you know him or not. One does not have to be righteous to be used by him. Our lives exist in Him and for Him. It is His plan and we are vessels. We are all used in someone else's test and walk. Satan is also being used. He was with me from the beginning, creating situations, downfalls, and roadblocks to pull me out of Yeshua's hands. God sets us apart from everyone to first take us down to humble us before raising us up. Some people are sent to Hades and back to give testimony for our benefit. Go through your trials holding on to God's unchanging hands. Anything He is doing in our lives is to deliver us from all sin, because we can not take it with us.

God let Satan build his kingdom using human beings because He knows anything that happens to us He will turn it around. Satan copies what God does in reverse. We have all been deceived; our eyes blinded until his kingdom was established. He uses things that affect the brain so that our minds will not be focused on him, and what he is doing. Intoxicated minds are not concerned about the mysteries of the heavens or the world. They enjoy being dazed and carefree. Sicknesses, illnesses, and diseases are used so we drown ourselves in pity living vicariously in a medicated induced state. He uses sexual immorality to confuse us and strip us of our identity. People do not know who they are anymore. Sexual sins, gender confusion, abortion, lasciviousness, and the like are all satan's works [Bible Gal 5.19-21]. We get caught up in his snare. He manipulates those who do not have discernment. He knows his time is coming to an end. Choose which God you will serve now.

This present generation is not God-fearing. They were not brought up in church nor have they read the bible. They are angry, fearless, and want answers but will not listen to reason. They are not aware of the works of the enemy so are easily drawn into his deceptions. Satan can only do what God allows. His kingdom will fall and all who come to Yeshua will be saved. Continue to believe in Yeshua and hold onto Him no matter what comes your way. Each of our lives has a purpose and we must walk in it. God's love is in control [Bible. Jn 3.16]. Biblical scriptures were included in this book to show there is a spiritual meaning to every issue.

Writing this book put me in a place to look at myself realistically in the flesh and ask am I where He wants me? With the stories I shared, I wanted to show how I did not walk a straight line but teetered off the path many times. My ups and downs come from the frustration of trying to figure it out myself. He always brought me back only after He let me fall and then chastised me for it. There are places I can not go, things I can not do, and people I can not associate with. If I waiver or fall, those I uphold will also fall. He chooses one from every family to represent them. Everyone is not held to this accountability. God does not call the qualified, He qualifies the called. He knows who will stand. Pay attention to the person in the family who is always talking about God and the Bible; they are positioned by heaven to bring you a message to set you on the right path. Ask someone for confirmation of what I am telling you. Research it for yourself. With love I leave this with you; I am not focused on where I come from, but where I am going. God's not through with me yet. The best is yet to come.

*Steering- To guide or control the course of [Merriam & Webster Dictionary]

*Forefather- Born before; older; plural ancestors. [Strong's NT 4269]

*Fornication- Surrendering of sexual purity; promiscuity. [Strong's Concordance 4202]

*Tithing- The tenth part. [Strong's Hebrew 4643]

*Vision- Appearance. [Strong's Hebrew 2376]

References:

Bible. King James Version. Online. Pandas of Caribbean Limited. Hong Kong Trade Center. Last updated 12, August 2021. Email: bibliaconsigo@gmail.com

Mirriam and Webster Dictionary. Online. Stanfy Corp. Copyright 2010-2023 Merriam-Webster, Inc.

Research:

Pillar College. Accelerated Degree Program: LEAD. B.A in Psychology, Counseling, Organizational Leadership, or Biblical Studies. 2001. info@pillar.edu.

Psychology Today. What's Behind Your Recurring Dreams?. "Theories About Recurring Dreams". Michelle Carr PhD. 2014, 14, November. Reviewed by Devon Frye

Strong's Concordance #4396. "A Prophet is an interpreter and forth-teller of the divine truth". Hebrew Usage: a prophet, poet; a person gifted at expositing divine truth.

Thayer's Greek Lexicon: Strong's NT 4396 cf. 4:16. "Hence, an interpreter or spokesman for God; one through whom God speaks". Cf.

USA.gov. Welfare Benefits or Temporary Assistance for Needy Families [TANF]. Last Updated 2023, 4, April.

VERY WELL mind. Mental Health News." Earliest Memories Start at
    Age Two and a Half, Study Finds". By Joni
Sweet. Fact Checked by Nicholas Blackmer. Updated 2021 28, June.
Wikipedia. org. Social Programs in the United States: "Overview of
    Social Programs in the United States". https://en.m.wikipedia.
    org>wiki>Social_programs_in_the_united_states
Yahoo.com. People Who Ask: History of Welfare in America. "What Year
    Did Welfare Begin in the U.S."

Printed in the United States
by Baker & Taylor Publisher Services